Are You Lovable?

Books written by Bjorn Stavness

Are You Free?

Are You Living?

Are You Lovable?

Are You Listening?

Are You Convinced?

This book contains hard fought after truths. For over 25 years I have ministered God's truths to free people from every imaginable stronghold. Not once a week in a counseling setting, but living alongside broken people for months, sometimes years, forcing me to turn my Biblical platitudes into life-changing truths.

Thank you, to the over 5,000 people that chose to search for God's wisdom in your time of utter hopelessness at the House of Decision, a woman's home, and the House of Opportunity, a men's home. What is written on these pages constitutes the liberating principles that God taught me and now share with you.

www.houseofdecision.com

Are You Lovable?

God's Love Rides on the Back of His Humility

Bjorn Stavness

ABUNDANT HARVEST
PUBLISHING

Are You Lovable?
Copyright © 2019 by Bjorn Stavness
Revised 2023

ALL RIGHTS RESERVED
No portion of this book may be reproduced, stored in any retrieval system, or transmitted in any form or by any means, electronic, mechanical, photocopy, recording or otherwise, without the express written consent of the author.

Editing/Formatting: Erik V. Sahakian
Cover Design/Layout: Andrew Enos

All Scripture is taken from the New King James Version of the Bible. Copyright © 1979, 1980, 1982 by Thomas Nelson, Inc. Used by permission. All rights reserved.

Library of Congress Control Number: 2019909338

ISBN 978-1-7327173-7-4
First Printing: August 2019

FOR INFORMATION CONTACT:

Abundant Harvest Publishing
35145 Oak Glen Rd
Yucaipa, CA 92399
www.abundantharvestpublishing.com

Printed in the United States of America

CONTENTS

Intriguing Thoughts 7

Part One:

Loving in Christ

1. The Father's Character...… ……………………....……... 10
2. The Father's Heart Revealed...…………………………..15
3. What is Humility?................... ……………………………..25
4. Love Riding on Pride's Back……..…………………….....30
5. God's Humble Design……………………………………..34
6. Fear of God……………………………………………….40

Part Two:

Humble Love

7. Best of All Possible Worlds……....….............................51
8. Humble God Vs. Proud God……. ……………….…...67
9. Seek My Face ……......………….......……………….............90
10. Tainted Humility..……………………………………..100
11. Good Enemy of the Best ………………………….…111
12. When Broken is Better………….............................124
13 Are You Lovable……………………………….…...139
14. Insulting Excuses……………………………….…..148

Part Three

Bones to Chew On

15. The Humility Factor..................................164

16. Learning Humility....................................177

17. Perfect Love Begets Humility.........................184

18. The Slow Death of Pride..............................194

19. Loving Muslims.......................................200

20. Lordship and Humility................................216

    Closing Acknowledgements

    About the Author

Intriguing Thoughts

When Jesus declared, "I am the light of the world," and "I am the way, the truth, and the life," and "I am the true vine," He was stating the many "I am" titles that describe His spiritual work in the world. (John 9:5, 14:6, 15:1)

Although Jesus claimed numerous titles, how many ways did Jesus describe His character in the same manner, using "I am" then stating His nature? How many of His character qualities, attributes like love, mercy, kindness, honest, generous, etc., did Jesus define Himself by?

It may startle you that the New Testament only records one time when Jesus described His nature, and He only referred to one of His many character qualities. That one special attribute should tell us something.

Jesus specifically declared, "Come to Me…for I am gentle and lowly in heart." In the Greek, "gentle" and "lowly" both mean essentially the same thing, humble. So, humble, wins the prize. (Matthew 11:28-29)

Naturally someone might ask, "Why be repetitive?"

The Jews used repetition for greater emphasis. For instance, if your heart found its greatest joy in giving to others in need, for emphasis you would express your character by doubling up on words describing "giving." You would claim, "Bring your needs to me...for I am charitable and generous."

What does it mean that Jesus never combined any other two qualities to describe Himself, like "I am loving and kind?" Or, "I am forgiving and full of grace?"

And what does it reveal that Jesus never even described Himself using just one character quality? Jesus never claimed, "Come to Me for I am loving," or "Trust Me because I am just," or "I am merciful." Only, "Come to Me...for I am gentle and lowly in heart."

Clearly, humility hit the bullseye at the center of Christ's nature. Jesus wore humility as His badge of honor. His humility gave His love the strength to set aside His rights in heaven as the Son of God to become a man. Not to come as a person in a high office of power and luxury, but as a man of very humble birth and treated as common. (Philippians 2:5-8).

Jesus submitted to His Father's leading and in doing so He humbly put others above Himself. The religious leaders even ridiculed Jesus for His "illegitimate" birth. His single greatest act of humility constituted taking on Himself the punishment due mankind. (John 8:41)

But Jesus' humility not only enabled Him to die to remove our sins, His humility empowered Him to take away our shame. Even though forgiven, one still looks in the mirror and says, "I know God removed the punishment of my adultery, but that only reflects on Him. Just because I am forgiven doesn't mean I am still not a horrible person-a shameful destroyer of my marriage and family."

To take our shame, Jesus died a dishonorable death, not as an honorable king. He hung naked, a fraud, guilty in the eyes of those He healed and fed, and laughed at by His accusers. His followers hid in the shadows with crushed hearts. His mother wept. He chose a shameful death, not the death of a king who nobly falls on his sword for his people. Why? To identify with our shame. *Being our shame bearer required unfathomable humility.* Isaiah 53

Jesus described Himself as humble because it was His humility that empowered His love to put a hostile mankind before Himself, costing Him His life. Hebrews 12:2

Without Jesus being humble, He never would have left heaven. Without His birth, there is no Christianity.

………………..

What about this wild question, "Is Jesus' Heavenly Father also humble?"

And this mind-blowing curiosity, "If the Father is not also humble, does Christianity celebrate day one?"

1

The Father's Character

Getting your mind wrapped around Jesus being the Creator of the universe yet humbly dying for a world full of hostile people will make your heart explode (Colossians 1:15-17). *However, and considerably more over-whelming, have you ever wondered, "Is God the Father also humble?"*

Crazy question? The Father of the universe, the King of Kings, humble? The absolute Ruler of all things, humble? There is no one above Him to humble Himself under. He possesses no weaknesses to be humble about. And the Father never voluntarily left His rightful place in heaven.

Humility doesn't really sound fitting for the Person Who rightly deserves everyone's complete reverence, appreciation, and obedience. Could the Father be humble even if He wanted to be? The question sounds self-contradictory, akin to, "Can God make a rock too big for Himself to lift?"

Consider these questions:

How could Jesus claim Himself humble and embody the perfect representation of His Father, if His Father is not also humble? And if His Father is somehow not humble, how could He direct Jesus to behave unlike Himself? How could

Jesus repeatedly proclaim that He and His Father are "one" if they aren't both humble (John 17:23; Colossians 2:9; Hebrews 1:3)?

Jesus scolded Philip, who asked Jesus to show him the Father, "he who has seen Me has seen the Father." Jesus represented His Father with "skin on." Every work Jesus performed characterized His Father's heart. Christ preached many times, "I came to reveal the Father to mankind." And, "If you want to know Who the Father is, look to Me." John 14:7-13

Further, we recognize how much a loving parent feels the same pain, if not greater, that their own child endures. Any loving parent would choose to endure an injury if it meant their child would not have to. If we, being selfish, identify intimately with our children's pain, how much more did Jesus' Father endure the pain and humiliation His own Son experienced, ordered by the Father Himself? "Love weeps with those who weep" (Luke 11:13; John 8:16-56, 10:30-38, 17:5).

Someone may think that perhaps the humility confusion between the Father and Jesus is answered if Jesus only put on humility for a few years and then, after His work was done, He discontinued His humility to get back to His Father's rightful nature.

If so, what other attributes was Jesus only putting on for those 33 years and then discontinued? His love? Mercy? Forgiveness? What other characteristics don't truly represent His Father?

Regarding heaven, Jesus promised those who faithfully served Him, "Assuredly, I say to you that he (Jesus) will gird himself and have them sit down to eat, and will come and serve them." Jesus continues to humbly serve in heaven. Luke 12:37

Suppose a believer prays, "Jesus, my new boss is out of control. Do I really have to submit?" Jesus answers, "Consider others as more important than yourself. Let Me exalt you."

The believer ponders, "Bummer, but hold on a minute. Why not ask God the Father, the all-business 'other' Parent, for His answer? He never washed anyone's feet. He transcends all mankind. He reigns as God Almighty. He declares, 'I am the head, not the tail!' And, 'I am a child of the King.' Surely, He will give me the option to throw my weight around!"

Imagine believing Jesus answers our prayers entirely different than His Father, as if the Trinity suffers from a split personality.

The Apostle Paul seamlessly connects the entire Trinity in one verse, making no distinction among Them, "But you are not in the flesh but in the Spirit, if indeed the Spirit of God dwells in you. Now if anyone does not have the Spirit of Christ, he is not His." Romans 8:9

In Luke 9:48, Jesus states, "Whoever receives Me receives Him who sent Me." What about Himself is Jesus asking us to receive? His humility. "For he who is least among you all will be great."

Jesus emphatically described Himself one time, humble. If any of His attributes were eternally true of Him, it reasons that humility stands out as that one. "Jesus Christ is the same yesterday, today, and forever" (Hebrews 13:8).

Jesus prayed to His Father, just hours before His cross, "I have glorified You on the earth…now, O Father, glorify Me together with Yourself with the glory which I had with You before the world was." The "glory" that Jesus gave His Father was the very humility that empowered Jesus to wash Judas' feet and will shine even brighter in a few hours on His cross. Jesus tells us how He defines glory, for Himself and His Father. John 17:4,5

....

God possesses transferrable and non-transferable attributes. His omni attributes, being all-present, all-knowing and all powerful are not transferred. All His character attributes are transferable.

Paul writes for us to spend the same selfless love as Christ, "Do nothing out of selfish ambition or conceit, but in humility consider others as more important than yourselves." How are a bunch of people born in their pride going to walk in Christ's humility if they don't first receive it from Him? Philippians 2:3

Again, Paul states, "...what do you have that you didn't receive?" 1 Corinthians 4:7 And James adds, "Every good and perfect gift is from above." James 1:17

Ironically, if we could manufacture our own humility, we would have something to boast about. Boasting never gets anyone close to the kingdom of God. 1 Corinthians 1:29,31, 13:4, 2 Corinthians 10:17, Ephesians 2:9

Clearly, the Spirit of Christ, dwelling in us, abundantly provides us with His humility as with all of Christ's character. John 14:26, 16:13,14, Romans 5:5

If the Father is not also humble, how do we reconcile Jesus enthusiastically distributing humility as He sits at His Father's right side? Is the Trinity divided on the one attribute that Christ described as His essence? Acts 2:33, Hebrews 8:1

2

The Father's Heart Revealed

Where do we find the Father's heart in fact displaying humility?

The Bible clearly states that God forgives only the humble and they, not the proud, will inherit the kingdom of heaven. If God Himself is not humble, then there exists a fundamental conflict of character between the Father and all those in heaven, including His Son (Matthew 18:4; James 4:6). Conversely, if God is prideful yet refuses to forgive the prideful, He rejects those of like character.

The Bible plainly teaches that to live pleasing to God we must receive both the desire and the ability to do so from Him. Further, we are commanded to humbly "esteem others better than" ourselves. Where does that humility come from if not from God (Philippians 2:3-4, 12-13)?

Toward the conclusion of Jesus' Sermon on the Mount discourse, teaching the multitudes to love their enemies and turn the other cheek, and a great deal more that requires supernatural humility, Jesus then summarizes His message with "you shall be perfect, just as your Father in heaven is perfect" (Matthew 5:48). Plainly, Jesus thought His Father's heart possessed the humility that His teaching required for obedience.

In Micah 6:8, God requires us to "walk humbly with your God." In Amos 3:3, we read, "Can two walk together unless they are agreed?" How can we walk in humility, together with God, if He is not also humble?

Again, shortly after washing the disciples' feet and just hours before the shame of the cross, Jesus prayed to His Father, "I have declared to them Your name, and will declare it" (John 17:26). Whose name? His Father's name. How? By humbly dying. Everything Jesus did and said was in obedience to His Father's leading. It is impossible to imagine His Father requiring humility of His Son without possessing humility Himself. *Undoubtedly, the Father's glory is found in His love's humility.*

At this point you may be asking, "But where does the Bible plainly claim God is humble?"

Psalm 113:5-7 states, "Who is like the Lord our God, who dwells on high, who humbles Himself to behold the things that are in the heavens and in the earth? He raises the poor out of the dust, and lifts the needy out of the ash heap."

The Father's humility carried His love out of heaven's gates, then stooping down, identified with the desperation of those in need. God doesn't throw nice things down from heaven. He comes down, bringing His heart with Him.

Like Father, like Son. Jesus "did not consider equality with God a thing to be grasped. Instead, He emptied Himself by assuming the form of a servant, ...He humbled Himself by becoming obedient to the point of death, even death on the cross." Philippians 2:6,7,8

Like Son, like Holy Spirit. Romans 8:26, *"Likewise the Spirit also helps in our weaknesses. For we do not know what we should pray for as we ought, but the Spirit Himself makes intercession for us with groanings which cannot be uttered."* The Spirit doesn't sit aloof, He feels our pain and prays for us when our pain overwhelms our faith. Galatians 4:6

In Genesis 2:18, God Himself declares Adam needs a helpmate. He then created Eve, someone to support and serve Adam. The Hebrew word describing Eve's role, "helpmate," is "Ezer." Ezer literally means "one who helps." The very role God gives Eve in Adam's life, "Ezer," God offers to fulfill Himself throughout the Old Testament. God names Himself "Ezer," for all those who call out to Him. "Ezer" embraces the same role between wife and husband today. Let that sink in for a minute. (Exodus 18:4, Deuteronomy 33:26-29, Psalm 70:5, 121:1, Ephesians 5:22,23, etc.)

The Father also declares He is a "jealous" God (Exodus 20:5; James 4:5). He deeply yearns for a relationship with us even in our rebellion, not considering us beneath Him. Only humility pursues someone after their kindness is coldly rejected and their office is disrespected, repeatedly.

His jealousy is love driven, for our sake, not a harsh attitude towards us. His heart aches over our loss in choosing another to serve, no different than a parent's heart breaks when they see their daughter returning to the man who abuses her or a son addicted to a drug that will inevitably destroy him.

Parents that love their children experience jealousy, wanting to pull their children back to safety because they desperately desire better for them.

Only a parent possessing a humble love endures the pain as they yearn for their child to come back to them after being rejected. Again, for their child's sake.

Our heavenly Father also claims His heart suffers long. He offers us His kindness to initiate a love relationship with us, but we often take His kindness as if it's owed to us and live as we please. In our continual ingratitude and defiance, He never vents His frustration by rubbing our nose in our disobedience. His broken heart doesn't seek payback. Instead, His heart continually offers us a way back (First Peter 3:9).

In our rebellion we also make ourselves spiritually unfit to receive greater blessings. Sadly, our Father must keep His infinite goodness pent up within Himself when He so strongly desires to pour more of Himself into our lives. His heart grieves as He sees us suffer the consequences of living apart from Him (Nehemiah 9:17; Matthew 23:37; Romans 2:4).

On a side note, the Father implanted His Spirit within us as a promise, sealing us with Himself as a pledge of His commitment to us. Imagine what His Spirit undergoes, being sealed into a relationship that listens to all our thoughts that we entertain that offend Him. Our unforgiveness, fears, lust, envy, and whining. Who willfully tolerates that ongoing disrespect without an infinite degree of humility (Psalm 139:1-6; Ephesians 1:13-14, 4:30; James 4:1-5)?

God always knew how little our hearts would comprehend His costly love for us and sadly, how little we would appreciate His love that we do understand. Instead of rejecting us for our foolishness, He patiently waits for us, eagerly desiring for us to accept His offer of a friendship. Clearly, His pursuing a friendship with us costs His heart far more than ours.

When the prodigal son returned home smelling like a pigpen, he only hoped to become a household servant. How did Jesus depict His Father? He came running to meet His son, greeting His filthy son with open arms, and carrying gifts. Who wanted the relationship more? It sounds inconceivable and reversed, but could the Creator of the universe be the one humbly offering... "It is My pleasure to have My son back." (Psalm 149:4; Jeremiah 23:23-24; Luke 15:20)?

....

Are you feeling uneasy about our heavenly Father being humble? Too much weakness? *Could it be that humility in God comes from a strength, not a weakness? Perhaps even His greatest strength and ultimate glory. His unsung hero?*

What are the "glory" rules in heaven? Jesus said, "Whoever exalts himself shall be humbled, and he who humbles himself, as this little child, the same is greatest in the kingdom of heaven." Humility equates to greatness in heaven.

And, "Anyone who welcomes a little child like this on my behalf welcomes me, and anyone who welcomes me also welcomes my Father who sent me. Whoever is the least among you is the greatest." Luke 9:48, Matthew 18:4,5

Not only is humility rewarded with greatness in heaven, the humility that welcomes Jesus welcomes His Father also. His Father loves humility no differently than Jesus because they are perfectly one in nature, here and there. John 1:14, 14:9,10, 2 Cor. 4:4, 6, Col. 1:15,16

And there is the matter of who God has chosen to represent Him, to bring Him glory. "…not many were wise from a human perspective, not many powerful, not many of noble birth. Instead, God has chosen what is foolish in the world to shame the wise, and God has chosen what is weak in the world to shame the strong." 1 Corinthians 1:26,27, Matthew 11:25,26, James 3:17

Paul does not say that God's power is made evident by our weakness as He does with Paul's thorn in the flesh. Paul reveals God's love for the "bottom of the barrel gang" and He isn't embarrassed by their inability to represent His supremacy, no more than a Lion is concerned with His reputation among mice. 2 Corinthians 12:7-11

One would think God would have chosen a far more impressive family if He wanted to bring our idea of glory to Himself. Unless, we got heaven backwards. What we think is lowly in the natural is precisely what brings Him glory. It is spiritually disjointed to imagine how something that brings Him glory (lowly people) does not also represent His nature.

God chose spiritual strength, not natural strength, to glorify Him. Our sin curse has corrupted what we esteem. We don't recognize what the Trinity considers worthy of glory.

When God chose us to be His children, He knew how incompetently we would succeed at the "doing" part. Our natural skills are embarrassing. He chose us to represent His character, and He loves it when He sees His strengths in us, however disrespected by the world. John 15:20

If humility was not an attribute of the Trinity, They must expect us to manufacture it within ourselves. If so, we are essentially earning the most critical condition of God's forgiveness. "God gives grace to the humble." Impossible. James 4:8

....

A common reason we struggle accepting humility as "baked" into God's agape love is born of our sin nature confusing His glory with our pride. We smirk at someone who brags after making the winning shot, "Hey, don't be a glory hog." Is God also an annoying "glory hog" when He demands all our worship? Unlike ourselves, His holy nature never turns His glory into pride. Proverbs 6:17

How could God glory in pride in Himself if He hates it in mankind? Is it because we have nothing to be prideful about in and of ourselves? Does God love pride only if justified? 1 Corinthians 4:7

We must understand that pride prohibits agape love. Justified or not, pride destroys the essence of God in God.

Merely because God asks us to measure our utter weakness against His greatness to help us trust in His ability to govern does not mean He possesses a smugness that enjoys building up His self-importance. The idea is lunacy. God does not compete with us, causing Him to rub our noses in our feebleness. Our pride does that with others. "Where were you when I laid the earth's foundations...." Job 38:4-41

We praise God for His holiness, but do we understand how His holiness purifies His love? God's holiness acts as His cleansing agent that puts the pure agape in His love. His selfless love places us before Himself. To reach us in our rebellion, His love, made selfless by His holiness, jumps on the back of His humility. Holiness produces greater glory to Himself, making a way for His love to love the naturally unlovable. We have His holiness to thank for making a way for His extravagant love to reach us. Romans 8:8, James 4:1-5

Jesus' humble love freely set aside His rightful heavenly glory because He possessed no pride to argue otherwise. Since the Father sent Jesus, His heart not just signed off on Jesus' mission, He initiated it. Even in Jesus' humble state, Satan never humiliated Jesus as Jesus was never controlled by Satan or defeated by death. Nor did Christ's cross humiliate the Father. Humility cannot be humiliated. However, "Pride goes before destruction, a haughty spirit before a fall." Proverbs 16:18   Phil. 2:1-10

....

We know that God has nothing to be humble about, but for God's love to reach us and far greater, to intimately identify with our pain and joy, He eagerly chooses to humble Himself, i.e., agape love.

Sacrificing His Son provides the proof that God humbly put us before Himself. And His love does not stop at "I forgive you, now you are on your own." *It deeply matters to God that our hearts live in peace, not fear.* Do we believe God's love walk through the fire with us? Our clear answer, "Well, He met us in our cesspool of rebellion, lifted us out, and put us on holy ground to live in oneness with Himself, now. I think God invented 'walking through the fire together.'" Romans 5:8, 8:31,32, John 17:3

Read how "low" Jesus states His "Most High" Father's love will go, "But love your enemies, do good, and lend, hoping for nothing in return; and your reward shall be great, and you will be sons of the Most High. For He is kind to the unthankful and evil." Luke 6:35

....

God created man in His image, which explains why we yearn for oneness above all else. Even though sin blurred our understanding of His level of oneness in a tragic way, we still long to love and to be loved back. Where did that deep desire for oneness come from if not from God? A sea sponge? Satan?

God remains complete without us. He desires to share His completeness with us, proving His love by humbly "feeling our pain and joy in His heart." *Now He is asking that we resist our pride, humble down and do the same towards Him, and with Him towards others.* Humility is a prerequisite for loving God back because humility is "baked" into His agape love. The only love compatible with His love embraces His agape love. John 3:16, 1 John 3:16

Although bizarre to consider the Father humble, the Bible makes many inescapable connections. By the end of this book, understanding the humility that carries God's love to reach us will bring you a greater respect for God's glory. And, change the way you serve others.

3

What is Humility?

Let us take a closer look at the basic nature of humility and pride.

We know all too well what pride looks like in ourselves and others…especially others. Pride makes us little gods, believing, "I trust myself on how best to love others and things. My judgments are right. I want and deserve a better life for myself and I strive to make that happen." Add to that a little gloating when things go well. So, the self-serving life begins, leading to weak and warring relationships. Experiencing upper hell remains inevitable.

Pride holds many largely unconscious attitudes toward others, such as, "I deserve as much or more than others. So, respect my boundaries." And, "I will get along with others as long as I don't give more than I get." *Pride naturally holds a high opinion of its own opinion and pursues control in order to live selfishly. Proverbs 3:5,6*

Our pride effectively defends itself with others (at least in our own minds), but defending our pride becomes absurd the instant God comes into the picture. Try "squaring up" against God, waving your fists in the air and announcing, "I am replacing You with me." Or, "I am going to mop the floor with You and your lousy decisions."

Reality quickly acquiesces, "You created the world, I did not. I make mistakes, You don't. You know all things, I do not. You are in control and I only pretend to be. You are invincible, tiny microbes eat up my body. And, where did I put my *bleep bleep* reading glasses?"

Although everyone quickly realizes they cannot compete with God, only humble people concede. "You are right and I agree. I admit that I depend on You living within me to create a new 'want to' and the ability to do anything of spiritual value. I trust You to do far more with me than I can. I yield to You, not command You."

Clearly, when in God's presence we easily understand how humility fits mankind, but we may still question how an infinite God could be humble about anything?

Unless, once again, humility in God comes from His love's limitless strength, not a weakness. Humility carries all of God's selfless attributes to reach us, reaching across our sin barrier that Christ's cross broke down. Humility is God's unsung hero, His rescuer that He does not spotlight but expects us to appreciate and become.

God's selfless love considers the needs of mankind over His own, without pride considering, "Am I getting as much as I am giving?" His love weeps with us in our brokenness, knowing we will never comprehend how He feels our pain greater than we do ourselves. He also knows many will angrily believe He doesn't care. Matthew 25:35,36

The boundless reach that enables the Father's love to pursue the murderer, rapist, homosexual, adulterer, liar, swindler, thief, and gossiper reveals how His humility comes from a strength. His love requires humility to power past all of mankind's anti-deserving behavior, including giving wisdom to the arrogant person who rejected it a thousand times before, and grace to the lifelong embittered churchgoer who refused to let go of an old offense until dying.

The Father's humility empowers Him with an unstoppable love that stoops down to love us, looking past His pain and our unworthiness. Christ's cross took away the sin of the world. *Then, the Father's humility continues to put a world far beneath Himself before Himself.* John 15:13; Romans 5:7-8; First John 3:16

....

Not so fast, you may be thinking, "Maybe Christ's humble cross and the Father's painful 'walking through the fire' with us only came about as Their undesirable 'Plan B.' Perhaps humility was an unwanted cost that mankind's sin required. Like a builder who regrettably must throw good money after bad to cover unforeseen expenses in order to complete a huge complex."

So, that reasoning goes like this, "God's initial creation in the Garden revealed His preferred cost of love. Like cuddling and feeding a cute puppy. But mankind got stupid and sinned, forcing God to regrettably reach deep into His love's emergency fund to get mankind out of his mess. Humbly paying for our mistakes constitutes God's bailout penalty for creating and loving a sorry pack of dogs that attack each other."

The Bible states that God knew mankind would sin and how much sin would cost Him before creating mankind. His humility existed before the foundation of the world, not after Adam and Eve rebelled. God, being all-knowing, knows the future. If sin caught God off guard, causing Him to resort to an extremely costly fix on the cross, what will Satan devise next to trip God up? God ceases to be God if Satan or mankind can manipulate Him. First Peter 1:20; John 17:5, Revelation 13:8

Maybe you just remembered, "What about Christ's cross making us His sinless children in the eyes of God? He even calls us saints because He sees us through the work of Christ's cross, not in our sin. If we are already made perfect in God's eyes, then His love no longer stoops down to love us."

Imagine God hearing one of His kids pondering, *"Since God made me His holy child, I do not offend Him when I harbor offenses against others. And if I treat others poorly, since I am perfect in His eyes, He cannot feel injured. I can lust and hate all day but He only sees my pure thoughts."* Romans 3:7,8

Because we know of His love and forgiveness, our intentional violation of His purity becomes a personal attack, amplifying the heartless nature of our rebellion. "…to whom much is given, much is required." Luke 12:48, Matthew 18:23 & 35; First John 1:9

If a student refuses to obey their school teacher, their offense violates their teacher's authority. However, when the teacher's own child refuses to obey, their offense cuts far deeper because it violates a love relationship.

Naturally, we think it cost God the most to forgive us our immoral behavior. The fruits of the flesh. We ignore the grief His heart feels when we fail to humble down to love others as He loves us. We often get rid of the "put offs" but do not obey His leading to "put on" what pleases Him. *We fall short of the "glory of God."* In Corinth, the one offense that God dealt with the harshest was neglecting the needy at communion, not their many immoral sins, etc. Romans 3:23, 1 Cor. 11:29-34, Eph. 4:24-32, Col. 3:1-14

When believers stop their ugly sinning, ridding their lives of the pain those sins cause, but refuse to obey their heavenly Father, God's heart suffers even deeper their willful and personal refusal to love Him back. His humility powers beyond their personal offense and lovingly disciplines them for their own benefit. Hebrews 3:10 & 17, 10:26-29

4

Love Riding on Pride's Back

Are you still unsettled whether God's love is humble? Someone might wonder if there remains a third option for God, other than humble or proud? 1 Peter 5:5

Jesus would have certainly distinguished Himself from His Father on this chief point. "When I claim My Father and I are one, I mean in every way but one. He is not humble. Instead, He is..."

In Proverbs humility and pride are opposites, with no mention of a more noble possibility to humility, "When pride comes, then comes shame: But with the humble is wisdom." Proverbs 11:2, 16:19, 29:23, (also: Daniel 4:37, Isaiah 13:11)

Could God's greatness, or wisdom, or power substitute for humility?

Humility and pride are attitudes, not abilities. A proud God uses His greatness, wisdom, and power to set Himself far above His creatures. A humble God uses His greatness, wisdom, and power to reach down and help His creatures. Proverbs states God hates pride, first and foremost on His list of seven things. Proverbs 6:16, 16:5

Just for giggles, let us imagine what God's love would look like if His love rode on the back of pride, or any version of pride:

Pride gives to get. Pride comes to be served, not to serve. Pride-driven love wants an upfront understanding that it gets back more than it gives or it moves on to someone else. God's heart, if prideful, would never have made itself vulnerable to the welfare of a weak and rebellious person.

Love, riding on the back of pride, demands, "You are here for my benefit, I am not here for your sake. Earn your keep." Fear then, not love, drives obedience. A prideful parent sets down rules to unilaterally benefit themselves, not to teach their children what is best for them. Consequently, their child's obedience comes from fearing the wrath of a vengeful parent, not an instructive parent hoping they will reciprocate a love relationship. "Perfect love casts out fear" (First John 4:18). Lamentations 3:32,33

If prideful, God could have devised a painful system to avoid rebellion by giving everyone the equivalent of a spiritual shock collar, like those used on dogs to shock them if they leave the yard or bark.

Instead, God's love desires what is best for us, not what protects His heart. God's heart feels the pain of our disobedience, the system His humble love devised and anticipated before Genesis 1:1. Jesus states that God judges mankind on the fact that He "feels everyone's pain, and joy, in His heart." Matthew 25:31-46

We are here to glorify the Father, as Jesus brought glory to His Father. And what would that glory look like? Exactly like Jesus. Once again, how did Jesus self-describe Himself? Humble. Our walking humbly brings glory to the Father. Hours before the cross, Jesus prayed, "And now, O Father, *glorify Me together with Yourself with the glory which I had with You before the world began.*" Love, riding on the strong back of His humility, predates creation. John 17:2-5

....

On the other hand, what would a man-made god look like? A prideful heart would naturally design a prideful self-serving god. A god that remains aloof, speaking from his indifferent heart he orders his creatures using fear of punishment as their motivation. He will talk about love, a love that responds to first being served. Not a weak love that initiates or gives far more than he takes. Definitely not a love that returns kindness for evil or willfully walks through the fire with his creatures.

A man-made god transcends all his creatures in ability and relationally. He takes pleasure in keeping that distance and tells his creatures to worship him for his power.

A man-made god would never put his creatures before himself. A man-made god would never speak of oneness. No one could ever be worthy.

A pride-driven man is attracted to a pride-driven god. Their self-worth grows as they work for their god's favor.

As a person becomes who they worship, a prideful person is given permission to love others selfishly.

5

God's Humble Design

When thinking about creation and God giving man the ability to grieve His heart by disobeying Him, consider this thought-provoking question: "What does loving an anti-deserving person reveal about God's character that can't be revealed by loving a merely undeserving person?" Or, stated another way, *"What did God reveal about Himself outside the Garden that He could not reveal inside?"*

Meeting our needs while living in the sinless Garden of Eden required a love based on giving kindness to someone undeserving. That was not enough for God. He wanted to bring greater glory to Himself by loving the anti-deserving, patiently caring for us while we facilitated in our rebellion. *The more anti-deserving the recipient, the more powerful the humility required and revealed to carry His love.*

God desired mankind to witness His selfless love to the fullest degree possible. His humility provided the strength required to pay the outlandish price His holiness required to offer forgiveness and restoration to all mankind. Christ's cross.

The Father knew some would gratefully respond to His grace, others would remain so self-absorbed that they believe they deserve forgiveness, while many more would not care. All of it points to a Creator who humbly wanted to reveal how much He loves us. "Longsuffering" truly represents His heart's nature (Romans 2:4, 5:6-8, 9:22).

God purposely fashioned a hostile environment toward Himself to undeniably prove the humble nature of His love. Merely loving a needy person (such as in the Garden) simply requires a generous love. However, being generous costs almost nothing when you are God. Simply say it and it is done. *Where is the evidence of love in something that cost you nothing? The recipient may be someone very likeable, like a playful kitten is easy to love.*

When it comes to choosing to care about someone who already has and often will reject your love, someone who willfully lives rebelliously, a far greater love is given. Not only does one give a gift without receiving anything back, *one's own heart becomes the biggest part of the sacrifice. The intended recipient rejected the person's invitation to build a relationship.* God intentionally put His heart in harm's way to expose His humble love for us. (Romans 8:6-7; James 4:4).

....

The following illustrates what God's humble love looks like in the workplace.

Imagine your co-worker, tormented by their nasty divorce, starts lagging at work. They make costly mistakes. They are rude to everyone. You feel terrible for them and pray, asking God how He wants you to help them. He brings to your mind to ask them if you can pick up some of their workload in this difficult time and if you can pray with them. Putting your heart out there promises to get messy, but you obey.

They say "yes," but the very next week their work performance gets even worse. When confronted by the boss, your co-worker blames you for their mistakes. You may get written-up or even fired. They gladly took your kindness yet returned evil.

Again, you pray, "God, what do You want me to do?" All you hear is, "Ask again." Only humility puts others before oneself instead of focusing on their ingratitude and unworthiness. Possessing humility, you grieve for them because they squander what is best for them. "I am still open to helping you. Are you ready to work together?"

As illustrated, the strength of humility needed to love others as God loves us is less about the physical cost required and more about the ingratitude and rejection of the person. Serving a grateful family member poses no problem. Serving the sleaze-ball at work who lies, gossips, and acts imbecilic—no way!

God's humble love is longsuffering, longing for a change of heart in the person who intentionally tramples on His heart. His humility keeps Him from saying, "Get lost, fool" when we live as though He does not exist. *Humility empowers God's agape love to full strength.* Our ability to love others on that level requires the power of God's humility within us. Matthew 5:10; Romans 5:6-8

God's love finds Him zealously raking the bottom of hell's sewers, waist deep in our prideful rebellion. He calls out, "Who wants to cleanse their lives of hell's torment and receive My love and forgiveness?" Who does God find at the bottom of hell's sewers? Those who lost their way. Who responds to His invitation? The humbled. He joyfully cleans them up and makes them His children. Who typically rejects His invitation? Preferring to live as their own sewer boss, the prideful, self-righteous person. Zechariah 3:1-8; Matthew 22:1-14; Luke 15:1-10; 18:9-14

That God would willingly allow His heart to become vulnerable, not just to our frailties, but also to our rotten behavior, characterizes the greatest mystery of the universe. *God's heart hurts when we hurt, even if our hurt is caused by our rejection of His help.* After we straight-arm Ezer, we beg Ezer to rescue us. And He eagerly does. James 1:1-5, 1 John 1:9

How can God identify with and endure the pain of the entire world? The same way that Christ identified with the sins of the world, taking them on Himself on His cross. Spirit to spirit. The essence of who we are.

....

God longs for oneness with us knowing we are virtually clueless about what a truly loving relationship even looks like. The Father readily opens His heart to someone after they have rejected Him countless times before. When we refuse His love, He weeps and implores us, and finally causes distress to those He loves in hopes of them coming to know Him (Nehemiah 9:26-38; Jeremiah 6:8; Luke 13:34; Hebrews 12:4-11).

God's humble love also makes His heart joyfully identify with our obedience to His love. To grasp that we can delight the heart of God represents one of the most incredible life-changing truths we will ever learn. Once known, revealing His humble heart towards others becomes the most exciting endeavors of Christianity. *"Whatever brings joy to the heart of God, that is what I have the strength for."* (Nehemiah 10:8 roughly reworded)

Sadly, spiritually speaking, we are all born on the war path against humility. Living selflessly, returning kindness for evil, and stooping to love the anti-deserving sounds ludicrous to our birth nature.

Ironically, God's humble love constitutes the strongest argument an unbeliever can form against Christianity. Nothing in the Bible is more irrational and unreasonable. And how many of His children represent His humble love to prove its existence and power? *Could it be that even Satan never believed God's humility possessed the strength to carry His love into man's putrid sewers to save mankind?* Matthew 4:1-11, 16:23; First Corinthians 13:12

After learning and experiencing God's humble love, we are compelled to love Him back. Then, in our obedience, His humility working through us makes us irresistibly lovable to

Him. *Just as declaring someone trustworthy represents a greater compliment than saying they are loved, for someone to declare us lovable embodies a far greater compliment than to call us loved.* Second Corinthians 5:14; Hebrews 10:32-39; James 4:6; First John 3:16

How lovable are you?

6

The Fear of God

The question is not, "Should we fear God?" But, "Do you have an unhealthy or a healthy fear of God?"

How we understand God's nature determines which we choose. If loving, we possess a healthy fear of God knowing we could never escape His correction in our sin.

Many times, throughout the Old Testament and more often than most realize in the New Testament, the fear of God is referred to as a reason for our obedience. Heb. 12:3-11, Phil. 2:12, 1 Pet. 1:17, 2:17, 2 Cor. 5:11, 7:1, etc.

An apparent contradiction arises, "Why do we told to fear Someone Who loves us?" 1 John 4:18

To begin with, the Bible gives numerous reasons to obey God, the chief of which is out of love. Other reasons include: bringing Him glory, creating a deeper walk with Him, receiving rewards in heaven, keeping a clear conscience, operating in faith, producing fruit, to have more to give more, the fear of God, etc.

Choosing any of the reasons stated, except for the fear of God, *moves us closer towards Him.* But when we obey out of our fear of God, we turn down sinning to avoid His future discipline. We are making a calculated decision to avoid pain. Instead of our hearts solely desiring to please His heart, our minds prudently determined it serves us not to sin to avoid God's inevitable "spanking." Duet. 28:15, Rom. 2:8,9

If fear of God's certain discipline discourages us from disobeying Him, then fear did us a favor, keeping us from straying away from Him and towards evil.

Back to the question, "Why fear God if He loves us?" What about God's nature resorts to using the fear of future pain to cause us to reconsider disobeying Him?

How could God love us and not hate evil for the devastation it causes us? God watches with contempt as evil effortlessly captures our attention and seduces us away from Him. His hatred towards evil, because of His love for us, moves Him throughout Scripture to warn us of His stern discipline that will follow if we fall for the seduction. Romans 8:7, James 4:4

Perhaps God would say, "If your love for Me does not persuade you to resist what tempts you, then forethought of My discipline should cause you to fear the pain if you go through with it. Wisdom fears the inevitable pain My love for you will bring if you decide to disobey Me. And, I guarantee that My love will catch up with your defiance. *You mock My love if you sin without fear."* 1 Cor. 11:30

....

Why is the phrase, "the fear of the Lord," often repeated throughout the Bible?

God desires we obey Him out of love, but our love starts spiritually broken. Born selfish, we don't comprehend pure love. Until our self-serving love matures into a cross-quality selfless love, our decisions remain selfishly pain-driven more so than love-driven. Our fear of God's adverse consequences appeals to our selfishness. Pain hurts. Romans 2:4

Think it through. Everyone wants to avoid negative consequences. If our love for God remains too immature to dissuade sinful behavior, God's unrelenting love for us should cause us to turn around. We contemplate, "Should I get even with them for hurting me?" Our flesh gives us a green light, "I figured out a way to hurt them without them knowing it was me. Awesome!" But before acting on our revenge, our fear of God forces us to reconsider, "Darn. God will know it was me. His love doesn't turn a blind eye. What will He do to me?"

"Catch me if You can," typifies the attitude of a person who scoffs at fearing God while acting on sin. They doubt His love.

Although attempting to outrun His loving discipline remains foolish, we often try.

When our love matures, we hate what God hates. Old thoughts of fondly entertaining sin are eagerly shut down without the need to fear painful consequences.

Godly fear serves the purpose of protecting us from our lingering foolishness that obeys our sin nature. When our spiritually immature hearts struggle to return God's love in the heat of a temptation, fearing how His holy love will "put the hurt" on us hopefully restrains us from moving away from Him. Hebrews 12:6,11

Fearing God's discipline could be illustrated by a protective fence. Imagine a youthful dog that becomes frenzied when kids walk by. The highly charged dog ignores his master's voice but respects the fence, barking wildly at the kids, running alongside the fence.

God, being a God of choice, made the "fence" low enough for a dog to jump over. The fence does not stop the foolish dog, but the sensible dog stops at the fence.

The unwise juvenile dog jumps the fence, choosing not only to disregard his master's voice and loving care, but puts itself in harm's way. That dog experiences "your sins will find you out" and His master's short leash as discipline. Numbers 23:32, Matthew 23:37,38

Hmmm...why would God need to discipline us if our choosing sin already punishes us?

Sin's consequences are punitive, God's discipline is restorative. Even after our hearts ignore our Master's voice and our minds disregard His painful discipline, God's love continues to hunt us down, desiring that we return to Him.

Sin, acted on or simply entertained, will cause anxiety, anger, depression, and many more upper-hell emotions. Those life-suffocating emotions initiate God's restorative discipline. God is indicating, "That feeling means you are going the wrong way. I am not the Author of anxiety." Our ugly emotions are His warning flags to notify us we went off-track in our obedience to His voice.

After we turn around and obey, He converts those emotions into His lower-heaven counterparts, peace, love, and hope.

....

Healthy and unhealthy fear of God:

When we grasp that God's love insists on His best for us, and His holiness hates the evil that destroys our lives, it makes perfect sense that He would bring agonizing consequences into our lives when we choose sin. Fearing that impending pain points to the fact that we recognize His goodness and should cause us to reject sin quickly. For hard-headed believers, it may take several failed attempts at trying to out-maneuver His loving discipline from catching up with them before repenting.

A person with an unhealthy fear wrongly believes God's discipline is punitive, taking His wrath out on them and happily rubbing their nose in their rebellion. They believe He considers them a menace. But Jeremiah writes, "Though

He causes grief, yet He will show compassion...For he does not enjoy hurting people or causing them sorrow." Lamentations 3:32, 33

When Christ suffered horrifically on His cross, the Father took out all His wrath against sin due mankind on His own Son. With God's wrath against our sin satisfied, mankind obtains oneness with God by accepting His free gift of righteousness. Prideful people believe their righteousness, not God's righteousness provided by Christ's cross, satisfies His wrath and earns His acceptance. Romans 5:9,10, 1 Thess. 1:10

The following illustrates how our view of God's character determines in what way we choose to fear God:

A father gave both his sons a bike to ride anywhere but warned them to stay away from the dangerous cliff. "Enjoy your new bike but if you disobey me, I will take your bike away." Since each son thought of their father differently, they interpreted his reason for his warning and their consequences differently.

One son complains, "My dad is a killjoy. He knows those cliff trails are the best. All my friends take chances and ride over there. He only loves controlling me to see if I will violate his demands so he can put the smash-down on me. No doubt he will laugh when he takes my bike away. Until he catches me, I will ride wild and free."

The other son reasons, "My dad sternly warns me because he knows how easily I am suckered into danger. If my love for him is drowned out by my love for riding dangerously, he hopes that at least the fear of losing my bike will keep me away from those cliffs. If he did not take my bike away, it means he does not value my safety. If he does take my bike away, it proves he cares more for me than me throwing a hissy fit at him."

Even in the Garden of Eden, where God's love could not shine brighter, Adam and Eve disregarded God's love when they ignored His "enjoy every tree but this one" warning. Instead of believing God's love would come after them in their rebellion, they believed the con artist, "You have nothing to fear. The consequences of eating this lovely fruit are rewarding, not painful. God is preventing you from enjoying life's best." Genesis 2:17-3:6

On the other hand, Abraham was made righteous when putting his son on the altar, "being fully convinced that what He had promised He was also able to perform." Abraham trusted in God's goodness, not his efforts, to keep His word on becoming a great nation. "…it was accounted to him for righteousness." And, "called a friend of God." Romans 4:20-22, James 2:21-23

Everything points to the fact that matters tremendously to God that we trust and obey Him knowing He is a good God, not a killjoy. A "rewarder of those who diligently seek Him." He strongly prefers we trust in His faithfulness. As backup, He knows our fearing that His love will catch up to our disobedience means we also recognize His goodness never turns a blind eye to our defiance. Hebrews 11:6

....

"How can God's love chase after us in our rebellion without compromising His holiness, even if His agape love has humility 'baked' inside?"

We have nothing within us to make ourselves right with God. Without God chasing us down to place His heart within us, our only option remains rebellion. Simply coming into the presence of God as God means little. Even the Adversary in Job came that close. By contrast, coming to God as Father first requires our accepting His offer of restoration. His "new birth." Job 1:6, John 3:3

Because of the work of Christ's cross, the separation that remains is from mankind to God, not God to mankind. That distance is bridged by belief, not works, proclaimed in both the Old and New Testement. Belief trusts God to make us righteousness; unbelief trust ourselves. Our belief in Him has His goodness "baked" in. 1 Cor. 1:30,31, 5:9-13, 2 Cor. 5:18-21, Romans 4:3, 11:20, Hebrews 3:12,19, 11:6

God's love chasing us down and our response to humbly trust Him are plainly illustrated in Luke 15, the "lost and found" chapter.

In Luke 15, Jesus gives three parables, each containing lost objects. A lost sheep, a lost coin, and two lost sons. All the parables illustrate how the Father's love enthusiastically pursues a wandering sheep, a helpless coin, and Father's love pursuing the lost elder son. In the third parable, Jesus also incorporates the need for our belief in His goodness by adding a lost younger son.

The elder son illustrates how our self-righteousness causes division between ourselves and the Father. Incredibly, the Father's love still pursues us in our arrogance. The younger son reveals our need to humble down and return to Him, believing His goodness will have us back. Equally incredible.

A quick review of Luke 15:

The Father's love travels after the thoughtless lamb that wandered off but remains incapable to find its way home. Instead of saying, "That stupid lamb, leaving me and my care, good riddens. It's just one," the Shepherd thought the "just one" wayward lamb valuable enough to leave the other 99 sheep. The Shepard treasures wayward sheep. Luke 15:1-7

The lost coin was diligently searched for as precious by its Owner. Even with the other nine coins in hand, the missing coin remained vital. The lost coin also remained powerless to find its way back. Luke 15:8-10

Unlike the lamb and the coin, the prodigal son acted willfully rebellious. Even so, His Father's love kept Him watching down the road, wearing his running sandals, longing to see his son return.

Pain, not love, caused the prodigal to humble down and return home. Without reserve, his Father ran and embraced him before he could get a word out. God's love still runs to us when our repentance is pain driven. Luke 15:11-32

The prideful elder son hated the grace extended to his disgraceful brother, relying on his own goodness. His pride divided him from his Father, but Jesus states no such division exists between his father and him. "But he was angry and would not go in. Therefore, his father came out and pleaded with him." Luke 15:28

God's love eagerly meets us in whatever humble state we are capable of repenting in, love driven or pain driven. Does our love also offer forgiveness to others, wearing our running shoes, hoping for their restoration? If so, God finds us lovable.

Not by accident, restoration immediately prompted a party in each parable. Too much too fast? One would think God would first require a probationary period to determine if their repentance improved their behavior. "Show beats tell."

When God makes us one with Him, He not only cleanses our hearts, He implants in us His new "want to." Not until after He throws His oneness party do we possess the power to change our heart's motives and behavior. Only then are we equipped to walk out what He worked in. "…to will and to do" His good pleasure. Phil. 2:12,13, John 3:3, Titus 3:5, 1 John 2:29

Part Two:

Humble Love

Jesus taught using stories.

"Jesus told the crowds all these things in parables, and He did not tell them anything without a parable." Matthew 13:34

This section uses stories to illustrate Biblical truths.

Enjoy.

7

Best of All Possible Worlds

Challenging Thoughts

When folks ask the question, "How can a good God allow so much pain and suffering?" typically someone answers, "If God enables a person with the choice to do a good thing to prove their heart's desire for goodness, God must also give the person the same opportunity to do an equally evil thing. If God made good their only choice, excluding the option for evil, no one truly demonstrates their heart's yearning for goodness. Consequently, we have people doing very sacrificial acts of kindness along with others doing horrific acts of violence."

Truthful answer, but it is stuck on the "math." Recognizing the equation that good and evil are both necessary outcomes of our free will is a side effect, not the chief purpose for pain and suffering.

Others answer, "Pain teaches us to rely on God. God uses trials to grow us into His nature. Like a mean co-worker teaches us patience. Pain and suffering mature us." Again, they are getting stuck on a secondary reason, found many times in the Bible, but it is not God's primary purpose (James 1:2-8).

Some answer, "A world full of pain and suffering provides the opportunities for God's kids to show His kindness and mercy to those in need. God wants His kids to reveal His loving nature to glorify Him." Again, this answer is fixed on an opportunity that pain and suffering offer, but that is not God's highest purpose (Matthew 25:31-46).

To understand God's purpose for suffering and injustice, we must focus on God's pain, not man's pain. God experiences greater pain and injustice than all mankind combined. Being finite, we cannot even start to imagine how God identifies with everyone's turmoil and injustice. But learning, *"Why God identifies* with everyone's pain and suffering" changes everything.

Who willingly creates a heartbreak that lasts thousands of years? Why would God intentionally put His heart in harm's way? Is He just a glutton for grieving or does He have a powerful reason He deems worth the cost?

Story One

As Dr. Rylie stepped into Denver's hospital room, Denver blurted out from his sick bed, "I feel like I got eaten by a bear and then pooped over the side of a cliff!"

Dr. Rylie smiled at his terminal patient, who was also his pastor. "Pastor Denver, are you really in that much pain?"

"No. I just like that expression but I am afraid to use it in a Sunday message. Nobody's mind will ever come back from imagining a bear sitting on the edge of a cliff, taking care of bear business."

Dr. Rylie nodded in agreement as he studied Denver's vitals. "So, are you planning on preaching this Sunday?"

"I think so." Jokingly, Denver added, "I've got a story about a doctor who must comfort people as he tells them they will not be breathing in three months unless God does a miracle."

"Are you going to break the news to the congregation?"

"After all the test results come back, yes, but I need God to give me a special word. Not for me; I do not fear death or dying. I just know when my people see me weak and losing weight, I will make suffering and dying all too real. Many will dread dying themselves."

Denver continued, "What concerns me is the subtle fear that people stuff deep inside about their own faith. Some will question if they will panic or lose their faith when it is their turn. Or they might even turn against God."

"Very true. I talk to many people who fear losing their faith when given terrible news. What will your Bible text be? I am looking forward to being able to share with others what God reveals to you."

"I don't have my message yet, but I think it is in John 15 where Jesus says, 'I have called you friends, for all things that I heard from My Father I have made known to you.' Jesus tells us what He is doing, even in our pain. I need Him to start explaining to me why we must endure such pain."

Dr. Rylie shook his head. "I guess you are expecting God to give His reasons for pain and suffering within four days, or you are going to look pretty foolish quoting that verse on Sunday."

"Yeah. I may need a backup sermon." Pastor Denver chuckled. "How about, 'I will be watching you all from heaven. If that doesn't keep you behaving right, I instructed Dr. Rylie to cremate me and take my ashes up in an airplane. When flying over your houses, I told him to flush my ashes down the airplane toilet. If my ashes floating everywhere doesn't keep you doing what I preached all these years, then I will tell God to give everyone hemorrhoids.'"

"Wow. I hope Jesus wants to be your friend and explain pain. You need to stay one more night and…I don't think airplane toilets work like that." Dr. Rylie left the room laughing.

That night, Pastor Denver knew he had to conduct serious spiritual business with God. His prayer went something like this: "Jesus, if we are truly friends, then I would like a few answers to encourage Your people through pain. All pain. Pain that hits when people hurt each other and physical pain. But not the standard 'free choice' and 'fallen world' and 'someone, somewhere, is worse off than you' answers that sound more like You are not in control and life is a crap shoot. I want them assured that You have a perfect reason for everything. They need a 'God is good, all the time' message that really holds up when going through pain that screams, 'God isn't good to me.'"

Surprisingly, the first thought that came to Denver's mind was when God turned the tables on Job. Job also wanted answers from God for his pain and injustice, got a little sassy with God, then finally God turned the questioning around and asked Job, "Hey bigshot, who is asking whom what? You've got this backward."

Denver realized he might have been looking at the question of pain in reverse. The question he should've been asking was, "What is God's purpose for pain and suffering, not first for me, but for Himself?" He needed to ask God to explain why He suffers pain.

Pastor Denver's mind first listed all the ways that God suffers for mankind. "When His Holy Spirit is resisted, He is grieved. When people reject the cross it breaks His heart. Oh, even the cross itself was extremely painful." Denver became very somber. "God's heart suffers with every thought and action of every person throughout all time that violates His nature. He also identifies personally and suffers with each victim that endures pain. But we think almost nothing of God's heartbreak. We are so spiritually dull and always whining about our own pain."

"But why all the agony for Himself?" Denver continued. "What could God possibly have hoped for to give man the ridiculous freedom to break His heart and still want a friendship? His purpose couldn't have been to enjoy a few minutes of harmony in the Garden of Eden and then live with a countless amount of grief for a few thousand years."

Again, Pastor Denver refocused on why God Himself experiences pain. He questioned God, "What is Your purpose for all Your pain in the grand scheme of things?"

With no one else in his hospital room, Denver dared to speak out loud as God's thoughts came into his mind. "To start with, you gotta really know My extravagant love because knowing it changes everything. So…the pain I endure works like a bright light to expose My amazing love to you. Without My suffering on your behalf, you couldn't see the incredible fine-brushed beauty of My love." Denver paused. He knew God was unfolding new understanding.

"So," Denver pondered, "Your pain and suffering magnifies Your love for me because nobody willingly endures a painful sacrifice to help others unless they love them. I get that. When I realize You walked through the fire for me on Your cross, I know for certain You won't back away from pain when it comes to loving me. I can trust You to walk through the fire with me again."

Then, as if God wanted to accept Denver's request to be friends, God ended, "More than anyone, I know how much pain hurts. My pain is your proof of My love for you because enduring pain for the one you care about proves love. For that reason, I purposefully added pain as My most potent ingredient that makes the world you live in the best of all possible worlds."

Denver's mind raced, trying to grasp what God was telling him he retraced his thoughts. "Everyone desperately wants God to convince them of His great love for them, so they in turn can trust Him. The pain He bears for us is His convincing proof of His love. If God made no personal sacrifice for me, how do I know He really cares? Not with gifts. Gifts are as free to Him as dirt. God's personal sacrifice, that cost Him part of Himself, tells all. This means that the greatest revelation we will ever have that He loves us embraces truly understanding the pain God's own heart endures for us."

"Then," Denver cautiously deducted, "it figures that the pain I experience, the hurt caused by others, gives me a greater realization of how much God went through and continues to go through for me. It also makes sense that my costly sacrifices work like a bright spotlight for others to see how much I love them. Pain is God's tool that lights up His love like nothing else can. I can also use pain the same way, lighting up how much God's love in me loves Him and others."

Shivers jetted down Denver's spine as he remembered how he matured spiritually. Denver admitted to Christ, "I remember after I first learned of Your cross…I grasped Your love in my head, but not much was going on in my heart…yet. But after others hurt me and I made them more important than my hurt, I got a little sample of the pain You experienced when You did the same for me. My heart learns to appreciate the fine brush strokes of Your love when I love someone beyond their offense. Our hearts are closely connected by love's pain. I become just like You."

Again, Pastor Denver rehearsed God's answer to "why pain" in his head. "You used pain to prove Your love. And when pain comes into my life, it is my opportunity to relate to Your love for me. Then as I obey You, to love others regardless of the pain they caused me...I become You."

"Wow," Pastor Denver shuddered, "did I just say 'I become You?' I don't know where that came from. Anyway, now I can piece together how God is good all the time. It's an upside-down, backward, gotcha trick." Denver wanted to practice his message out loud to make sense of how God's pain is our greatest proof of His love for us and how our enduring pain is His proof of our love back.

In the privacy of his room, Denver started his message by proudly announcing, "I have solved the problem of pain. There isn't any problem! Our real problem is first getting our minds wrapped around God's pain. Let me explain," Denver waved his arms as if preaching. "God decided, before creating us, that He wanted to show off His great love. Not the cheesy friendship kinda love that runs away when things get ugly, but the kind of love that gets strong when things are hard. God's love reaches past all our rebellion even though we break His heart again and again."

Imagining himself walking around the front of his church, Denver explained, "Who in their right mind intentionally creates a world where people would cause them pain? I mean enormous heartache. The kind that rips your insides out.

Every angry and mean thought we think and do injures God's heart. When He could squish everyone like a bug, He still forgives and wants a friendship with us." Denver paused, then sighed. "We must try to realize, deep down at the core of our being, how much God's heart willfully chose to suffer to prove His love for us."

"Once we absolutely, positively, know that God's love is not afraid to endure pain on our behalf, we can connect the dots. Understanding that His love is stuck on us when guilty as heck, we can certainly grasp that His love won't run and hide when we are innocently hit by a crisis. Like facing death. But, if we get caught up on hating our pain before absolutely knowing how much His love will endure for us and with us, we miss the mind-blowing peace that He will hold us tightly through our terrible difficulties."

Denver thought about their response. "You may be asking, 'If God wants to show off His crazy stuck-on-us' love when we sin, fine, but why do we have to get hurt as well? Why doesn't He pick on someone His own size? And we would thank Him even more for not beating up on us. Why did He have to include us in His sadistic 'show and tell' world of pain? It seems like a loving God would figure out a way to make a world where everyone plays nice and no one needs to get sick.'"

Pastor Denver grinned and replied to his own questions, "Great questions! I can think of two reasons why God wants us to also experience pain. Clearly, we can't empathize with His pain unless we also feel pain. Just like parents finally figure out how much their parents loved them as they struggle to raise their own rebellious child. And second, just as God uses pain as His bright light to reveal His relentless love for us, it is primarily through our pain that we show the same relentless quality of love back to Him and others. Pain tells all because enduring it proves who we make more important."

Pastor Denver continued, "Think about the 'who we make more important' part. Jesus could have said to His Father, 'Die for these rebellious ingrates? Are You kidding? This costs way too much to get far too little in return. If I don't mean that much to them, then they don't mean that much to Me.'"

Denver kept preaching, "But, instead He said, 'Whatever it takes, no cost is too high, I will pay it. Their ungrateful response doesn't cause Me to reconsider, it only saddens My heart.' Our offenses and indifference give Him the perfect opportunity to show off His selfless love for us now. Jesus even considered it a joy to suffer to reveal how much more important we are to Him than the heartbreak and physical pain He suffered."

"Knowing all that, if we really wanted to end all our arguments about 'why pain,' try explaining Christ's cross for two minutes..."

Denver paused from rehearsing his sermon to reflect, "This pain message is sounding very challenging, but there is no way my people are going to throw tomatoes at a guy with only three months to live. Now is my opportunity to really hammer um."

"So, you have one of two options to choose from. Option one, a selfish God who refuses to go through pain on your behalf because His love is too cheap. Logically, to avoid being hurt by our bad behavior, He necessarily makes us all idiot robots that can do nothing wrong. As robots we have no idea if He really loves us because all He gives us costs as much as a box of rocks. But at least pain doesn't exist for anyone."

"Or, option two, a selfless God Who willingly chooses to endure extreme pain to prove how much He really cares for us. Option two comes with pain for us so we can appreciate His pain caused by us. He also expects us to love Him back regardless of our pain. He obviously treasures His crazy quality of love and wants it coming back from us. Option two also means we overcome hurtful offenses to show God's crazy love to those who hurt us."

"Well, your choice of options doesn't really matter because you are stuck with a God Who loves you a ridiculous amount. To prove His love, He will suffer a great deal more pain than we even know exists. And if we never knew pain, God would be cheating us of the greatest blessing He can give us…becoming one at heart with Him."

"So, before you get hit with a crisis, you must first unquestionably know that God meant for the pain we cause Him to reveal His overcoming love for us. Pain is His 'proof of love' tool, not a dreadful mistake. If we love Him back like He loves us, then we say to Him what He says to us, 'You're more important to me than the pain I feel.' Supernaturally, our hearts identify with His heart and we become Him. Afterwards, we understand how God created the best of all possible worlds using pain."

As he lay on his hospital bed, facing the reality of his body dying, Denver wanted to make sure he prepared his people for the worst. "I need to keep this real. Knowing the 'why' of pain doesn't reduce the pain itself. Our hearts still get crushed by others. We still get sick and die. Our minds get weak when we are sick, so we may have moments of doubt. Yet, in our pain that we didn't choose, we know that God actually chose heart-wrenching pain to prove to us He isn't afraid to also endure our pain alongside us. And, through our pain, we understand how much it cost Him to love us."

Laying on his hospital bed next to his bedpan, Denver smiled as he closed his message, "I know this is a hard message and a little confusing, so I want your feedback. If you have a concerning question or even a criticism, please fill out one of our comment cards and place it in the box as you leave. This weekend's comment box is shaped a lot like a bedpan."

Summary

Countless millions adamantly criticize God's governing of the world. "Too much injustice and suffering." Many resort to believing God must have created this planet in good shape and then left. They reason He can't be a monster of a God because He is not directly responsible for the evil that happened after He left. But He remains a heartless jerk for abandoning His creation, something like a cold-hearted mother that abandons her toddler on the side of the street to fend for themselves.

Others reason it takes a stronger, more honest person to reconcile all the pain and injustice by believing there is no God at all. "Better no God than an evil God. Who needs Him anyway? Frankly, if He existed, even light-years away, He still has more blood on His hands than a million Hitlers. Better to just cross Him off your list and put on your 'big boy pants' and make the best of this dog-eat-dog world."

How does the Bible reconcile a loving God with all the suffering, injustice, disease, and death? Did sin unintentionally trash God's perfect creation and we deserve this mess? Is free will really God's best answer to pain? How is today's world the "best of all possible worlds?"

The dreadful problem of pain and injustice converts into a blessing when understanding the best of all possible worlds is the place where all the attributes of God are not just visible, but shining their brightest.

What would that world look like? Conceivably very beautiful contrasted by very dreadful. The sin that causes pain provides the necessary horrible backdrop for God to reveal how spectacularly bright His attributes truly are (Romans 5:17-21). *The greatest revelation we will ever have that He loves us embraces absolutely understanding the pain God's own heart endures for us and with us.*

Jesus revealed His great love using the appalling backdrop of His cross. In doing so, He revealed the enormity of His love. "You knowing My love for you matters more to Me than the pain I endure to expose it." (see Titus 3:3-6).

In the Garden, God would patiently deal with our physical limitations and our lack of understanding. Rather easy, frankly. But outside the Garden, He patiently and painfully waits on our surrendering our rebellious wills over to Him. And since we are typically pain-driven, not love-driven, He sadly must resort to using painful circumstances to get our attention. Nonetheless, His patience is not waiting with a begrudging attitude, keeping score of our rising indebtedness or our unworthiness to Him.

God humbly puts us and our well-being above His own. Paul reminds us in First Corinthians 13:7 that love "endures all things" (see also Romans 2:4 and Hebrews 4:14-16).

This very dark world is precisely where God's love shines the brightest because it costs Him the most to reveal His character. Now, when questioning how God could be a good God, one simply considers the pain He endures when we grieve His heart and the heartbreak He suffers when He identifies with the world's pain. *When walking in God's shoes, the existence of pain verifies His goodness.*

If we insist on convincing answers regarding pain, only "walking a mile" in God's shoes will provide them.

Afterwards we will begin to appreciate His love. Then our whining starts to turn into amazement. Eventually, if we dare to compare, we find God's humble love costs Him ridiculously greater pain than any pain we will ever face.

Learning how God intentionally chose pain to make known His love changes us. We catch onto the fact that the very thing that makes us angry with God and others is the very thing that proves His goodness. God does not deliver us from "the valley of the shadow of death." He walks through it with us, "I will fear no evil, for Thou art with me."

We see those who cheat us, offend, and lie to us differently. Those cruel people just became our opportunity to intentionally expose the beauty of God's love. The same dark backdrop that reveals the glory of God just became our dark backdrop to reveal God's glory through us.

God's humility allows Him to use evil as His asset to reveal His agape love. Will we?

One thing remains certain. We will not experience oneness with God until we embrace His costly quality of love and share it. Pain, like wind to a sailboat, can compel us to go in the direction of the nature of God and turn our suffering for good. Or, without Jesus the very same wind can take us to the jagged rocks of fear, anger, and self-pity. The choice is ours. Pain is simply God's tool to the end of bringing glory to Himself. (Joshua 24:15).

Don't blame God for being a glory show-off. Anything less would be unloving. *His loving us despite the pain, our proof. Our loving Him back despite the pain, His proof.* Best to stop whining and start walking in God's shoes.

8

Humble God vs. Proud God

Challenging Thoughts

The greater the sacrifice, the greater the love.

To pick up someone's dropped pencil is nice, but it says little. To offer to give them your last dollar, your valuable time, or something of major personal importance tells an underserving person you care about them. Nonetheless, and infinitely more powerful is the selfless love that sacrifices their life to restore the anti-deserving (Romans 5:5-10).

Additionally, we know that if we make the first move in hopes of restoring a relationship full of animosity, our offer most probably will be flatly rejected. "Once you were alienated and hostile in your minds expressed in your evil actions." Col. 1:21 CSB

....

Now, let's compare a proud God against a humble God: "What degree of sacrifice would each demonstrate to reveal their love to Their creatures?"

First a proud God:

A proud God proclaims the obvious, "You are far beneath Me. Consider it your highest privilege to make sacrifices for Me. Disobey Me and I can make life hell for you. If I don't, consider that mercy." A proud God treats His creatures as expendable tools that work to please Him. His pride feels satisfaction in getting revenge. He honors His reputation by "throwing His weight" around.

Just the idea of offering oneness with Himself remains absurd.

How does a prideful God demonstrate love? "I am abundantly kind and forgiving and generous as a reward to those who prove their devotion to Me. Being all-powerful, I am never vulnerable to being hurt by the behavior of My children." *All His attractive character qualities, mercy, forgiveness, kindness, patience, etc., are used as currency, given in exchange for service due Him.*

His love rides on the back of His pride and only travels to places that revere Him. Their sacrifice gives value. Fear of punishment hangs over the heads of all those who do not worship Him.

A proud God does not weep with those who weep, or rejoice with those who rejoice. Returning kindness for evil is considered a humiliating weakness, meant only for beggars who desperately attempt to win a rich person's favor. Naturally, His worshipers treat others with the same conditional love and harsh consequences as He treats them. (First John 4:18).

The behavior of a humble God:

By contrast, a humble God urges, "I offer My friendship to all without first measuring their worthiness. I need no proof of your devotion before extending My love to you. I will take the initiative, making any sacrifice to make our friendship possible, knowing full well you may reject My open-hearted invitation to a Father/child relationship." Matthew 5:45, 1 John 4:19

"It breaks My heart, for your sake, when you refuse My offer of a relationship. I am grieved that you will suffer the painful consequences of living apart from My care and direction. If you reject My selfless love, or refuse to give it away, I will lovingly discipline you for your sake."

A humble God takes His love to hostile places in hopes of serving helpless people. In return, He desires them to find oneness with Him and others. If they refuse His offer, His heart is grieved. He knows He is God, and like a lion, He has no concern for maintaining His reputation among mocking sheep. (John 15:15; Hebrews 12:10).

A humble God reveals His selfless love first, providing an endearing "hook" to draw worshippers to love Him back. When one of His children are tempted to disobey Him, His love uses fear of discipline. He hopes future pain will dissuade them from harming themselves. A humble God pays the price of placing others above Himself and expects the same behavior from those who follow Him (First John 4:10-19).

Choose your God, fulfill Their respective expectations and become Who you worship. A "Me before you" self-serving God or a "you before Me" selfless God.

Story Two

Sometime in the middle of the night, Denver woke up to the nurses hurriedly wheeling a man into his room who had been shot. Denver overheard the nurses talking about the emergency room being full and using Denver's room for overflow.

As the nurses left, Denver heard his new roommate swearing under his breath. Concerned about his new roomie, Pastor Denver asked, "Is there anything I can get you? Want to watch a movie or something?"

The man interrupted, "I loathe terrorists. They have no souls. They tried to murder at least ten people in cold blood."

Denver turned on the TV and found the breaking news. The cameraman attempted to expose the bloody crime scene as a reporter explained, "One or multiple gunmen opened fire on a group of people coming out of a movie theater after a late..."

Denver's roommate cut in, "I didn't see their faces, but two people wore dark clothing, had automatics, and shouted in some language I couldn't recognize, but I am certain I heard, 'Allah.'"

Denver introduced himself, "My name is Denver. How bad are you hurt?"

"Sergio," he responded. "I got a bullet in my thigh. Lost a lot of blood before the medics could safely treat me. It hurt, but they gave me some kind of painkiller. I just hope those two shooters are dead and nobody ever hears their names. They are cowards."

"Well, it is impossible for a country to rise above its religion. If you want to know what Muslim's believe, look at a Muslim country."

"Yeah, I think all religion—here, there, and everywhere—is about weakness. Instead of taking care of business for themselves, people like to pretend there is a God to either cry to or to excuse their horrific behavior. Everybody just needs to grow a pair and deal with life's difficulties."

Pastor Denver thought about Sergio's condemnation of all religions. "People argue about Islam and what the Qur'an teaches, but they can't argue about what it produces. Muslim countries are war-torn from civil wars that never stop. Fear and revenge are a way of life. If they don't have a strong dictator in charge, they will often destroy each other. All that in spite of the fact that their countries have boatloads of oil money and should be the most beautiful and charitable countries in the world."

Sergio added, "And, since I pay my taxes, which funds our military, I am considered at war with Muslims because we send troops and weapons to protect whoever is getting their butts kicked. And, that makes me fair game to shoot and kill in cold blood."

Denver responded, "No country can rise above what it believes. Obviously, the United States has its own share of violent terrorists, people troubled over injustices, whether true or not. But on the whole, if a country believes in a loving God, they love people. A merciful God creates a merciful people. A detached God, a detached people. A vengeful God, a vengeful people. Whoever their God is in their book, sometimes distorted by their leaders and teachers, that will largely determine who their people become."

Sergio shot back in a caustic tone, "I was raised an altar boy. I know firsthand how jacked up my priests were. And with all the evil in the world, I decided it best to handle life on my own. Right now, I have a score to settle. These fools tried to take my life. They need to pay."

"I don't know what you have been through, but your 'growing a pair' is going to cause you far more pain than that bullet. Our job is to forgive; the government's job is to bring justice."

"Are you telling me that you would forgive someone who just proudly shot-out a bunch of innocent people and tried to kill you?"

"God would tell you to forgive."

Sergio scoffed, "Easy for God to say 'forgive.' I am the one with the bullet hole in my leg."

"No, not really. Don't you remember the crucifix? It was far harder for God to say 'forgive.'"

Sergio grew angry by Denver's reference to the crucifix. "That's precisely why I decided to part ways with the Church. I will tell you who needs the crucifix…the priests that grabbed kids' balls and the terrorists that tried to shoot mine off. Frankly, neither of them deserves forgiveness."

"My bad," Denver apologized. "I am expecting you to do something that you can't do. If you don't have it in you, you can't give it away." Denver continued, "I give away what is in me. The shooters gave away what was in them. Sergio gives away what is in Sergio. Which, right now, sounds like revenge. And, like in the Middle East, and our domestic terrorists, revenge destroys everything."

Very confident of his argument, Sergio came back, "Violent people respect nothing but force. Which is why we need a huge military. Like you said, they require vicious dictators who will cut heads off if anyone looks at them cross-eyed. My way is to force a bunch of heartless killers to never kill again."

"I fully understand your reasoning. Violent people often only respond when forced, but your attitude makes a huge difference in what you do and how you go about it. God loves all people, evil people included. God wants even evil people to have a change of heart, not simply kill them. Whether a terrorist or a priest. Or even you and me for our bad behavior. Our job is to hope the best for them and God uses the government to bring justice for their actions."

Pastor Denver continued, "It all comes back to what is in you. I know that just me in me will really make my life miserable. I would become a hater. I know that God in me is my only hope for making the best of this crazy world. Knowing His nature is step one. Obeying His nature makes me appreciate God, and I even look forward to dying."

Sergio's mind began to race as he thought over Denver's words. He felt cornered by his own words. Sergio filled in the blanks. His anger and bitterness toward the Church ruined a big portion of his life, much like the war-torn towns in the Middle East. Now he faced another huge reason for bitterness to ruin a great deal more of his life. It suddenly dawned on him that he hated people who were filled with hatred, which obviously included himself, even if he was just seething on the inside. He was becoming a terrorist at heart.

Wanting to divert the conversation away from himself, Sergio asked Denver what he meant by "obeying God's nature makes you appreciate God?"

"It's true with anything, really. Not until my son raised his own rowdy sons that exhausted his patience did he appreciate my patience when raising him. Not until you learn to play the piano do you fully appreciate hearing a master pianist play. Not until you and I forgive those who hurt us do we really appreciate God's forgiveness of us. It's true with every attribute of God. They get real and powerful after we obey them."

"So, you're saying the only part of God that I appreciate is the part I obey?"

"Yep, to any degree. When I am generous, it becomes clear to me how generous God is. It's like we become partners in it."

Sergio added, "So, if I decide to take the crucifix and forgive evil people, God's forgiveness becomes real to me. I get how much He forgave me and I get rid of my anger?"

"Right. You become a certain kind of person by the beliefs you live by. You and I see and experience evil, but the terrorists, foreign and domestic, know evil even greater still because they harbor it. Only Jesus gives everyone the option not to live in the grip of hatred that continues the vicious cycle of loathing and vengeance."

Denver threw a question at Sergio, "Do you like the person you have become?"

Sergio thought for a moment, then answered, "I know my anger is justifiable. But these terrorists got me thinking about where their anger took them and where mine will take me. I don't want to become anything like them, justified or not."

"Well, you've got options." Denver turned off the news and yawned. "I am glad you are not hurt worse. I got cut wide open today, or yesterday now, and I really need some sleep."

Summary

This summary throws punches every direction. Get ready for your religious notions to take a few bloody hits.

Christians answer those who criticize Christianity as a hostile religion with, "The Bible is like a person. If you torture the Bible long enough, you can twist it up to make it say anything you want."

When criticized as a hostile religion, Muslims also argue their Qur'an is being manipulated by Islam haters. How can we get past the "spitting contest" on both sides that will never bring resolve?

Answer: Question which religion considers others as more important than themselves, even those who do not worship their God? Which religion presents a God who makes His heart vulnerable to being rejected and grieved? Which religion worships a God that makes huge sacrifices for those who defy His authority?

Both worship a "great" God, but what makes Him great remains polar opposite. Bottom line, which religion passionately worships a proud self-serving God and which passionately worships a humble others-serving God?

Take a quick look at the Biblical concept of God and the Qur'an's concept of Allah:

The Biblical concept of God is selfless, i.e., Christ came to serve, not be served. The Father sent His beloved Son to die for our sins. Jesus preached to return kindness for evil, as He soon would do Himself on His cross. Jesus loved the "bottom of the barrel" members of society. Those who could do nothing to pay Him back.

Jesus represented His Father perfectly. God loves the entire world, even those who reject Him. He makes the sun to shine on the just and the unjust. Jesus died for all sinners, even those who deceive and preach against Him. His heart yearns for us. God's love does not seek its own. He weeps with those who weep. When we walk back to Him, God runs towards us (Matthew 25:31, Luke 15:11-31; Second Peter 2:1).

The essence of Christianity goes far beyond knowing God loves us selflessly. Jesus prayed that we would live in oneness with Him, which first necessitates His selfless nature indwell us. We are born selfish, so we must be "born again" spiritually to have His selfless love in us to work out. Through our obedience to Christ's leading, we love others selflessly. We share the same oneness we experience with Christ with others (John 3:3, 17:23).

Christianity first requires a heart implant and then an exchange. God implants His new heart within us, we then exchange our old selfish "want to" for His new selfless "want to."

Since His Spirit dwells within us, God judges our hearts, not our actions in and of themselves. Right being must precede right doing. When someone acts kind for selfish reasons, God is not impressed. Being honest because it pays to be honest is no longer being honest. Everything Christians do must be driven by our desire to please God's heart, not selfish gain or earn our way into heaven. There is no fear in a love that loves unconditionally. Even our desire to live selflessly first comes from Him (Matthew 5:5; First Timothy 1:5; Titus 1:15).

Does God really love us at the expense of His own heart? Is He really a jealous God that yearns for His loved ones back? One more Biblical illustration:

God wanted Hosea to identify with His anguish over the nation of Israel's unfaithfulness. What did God ask Hosea to do to illustrate His pain?

Did God tell Hosea to start a farm, then get ripped off by unfaithful farm hands and finally whip them to make an example of them? Or have unruly children and punish their rebellion by disinheriting them? Perhaps make an investment, get defrauded out of all his money, then throw the crooks into debtors' prison? None of the above.

To empathize with His pain, God required Hosea to do something far more personally devastating. Hosea had to marry a whore to love and treat faultlessly. Not marry a virgin who already proved her faithfulness to her future husband. Hosea must have thought, "Surely my wife will cherish me and honor our marriage after she enjoys my kindness to her." Unsurprisingly, his wife Gomer cheats repeatedly on Hosea, tearing his heart out.

That vulnerability represents the humble nature of God's love. God married a prostitute, hoping His love would change her heart. Israel's unfaithfulness grieved God enough to want someone else to experience that heartache before qualifying them to express His broken heart to the nation.

....

The Qur'an states that Allah has 99 "most beautiful" names. Muslims are told to memorize them and use in prayer. (Most of Allah's names also reflect the God of Christianity.)

Allah is called the God of mercy, love, forgiveness, wisdom, strength, guidance, and many more. Allah possesses three names for forgiveness because He loves to forgive. Muslims worship Allah, bowing east to pray five times daily, and follow his commands. Allah is all-knowing, but does not dwell within Muslims. Muhammad was Allah's last (14th) anointed prophet and must be obeyed. Muhammad lived in fear of possibly not living up to Allah's expectations. Jesus is also referred to as a prophet and the only person ever born sinless (Qur'an 19:19).

The Qur'an reveals a God full of love and eager to forgive. However, mankind's sins are not paid for by Allah, Muhammad, or Jesus (Islam does not teach Jesus died on the cross. A martyr secretly took His place). Without a redeemer, sins are forgiven by praying for Allah's kind mercy, coupled by the complete obedience of the person sinning. Enough good works means forgiveness. Without a savior, forgiveness must be earned and fearfully pursued.

Allah's chief unforgiveable sin remains worshiping another God other than Him. Allah has no son or Holy Spirit. In support of one God, Muslims quote Deuteronomy

6:4, "The Lord our God, the Lord is one!" (The Hebrew word for "one" is "ehad." The same word used to describe Adam and Eve when they became "one" flesh. "Ehad" typically referenced only one, but did not exclude a compound one, as with Adam and Eve. Genesis 2:24)

Allah wants worshipers and gives His followers much to worship Him for. Yet Islam does not reveal a God who stoops down to become a man and serve, one who suffers and dies for all people, including those who rebel against Him. Allah does not return kindness for evil, or kindness for nothing. Allah does not humbly initiate. He pours out his love on those who first love him. (An impossible option in Christianity. The love needed to love God back with must remain selfless and He is our only source for such love.)

Without a Holy Spirit, Allah does not reside within His followers. He is after their actions, not their motives. Since a selfless heart is not given or expected, good behavior driven by selfish motives does not raise any red flags.

Some obvious questions arise. With all of Allah's 99 beautiful names—provider, guardian, generous, source of peace—why don't his worshipers "provide" oil tankers filled with humanitarian supplies to a terrible natural disaster in a non-Muslim country? Where are the Muslim planes "generously" feeding the starving kids in India? Why are Muslim countries often at war with each other, heartlessly killing men, women, and children? Why don't Allah's worshipers show kindness to other religions in their Muslim countries, instead of proudly persecuting them? Where are the "guarded" Christian churches on their street corners or Christian women "peacefully" walking freely in their own dress?

Where are all of Allah's 99 names, Most Gentle, Forbearing, Affectionate, Friendly, Merciful, All Protecting, etc., being lived out towards the hurting people around the world? Or towards those in their own backyard who do not share their belief in Allah? (Qur'an 59)

As with all religions, some who claim to be Muslim are not truly Muslim. Yet countless Muslims do worship Allah, praising His 99 names often, but show little or no charity. The reason true Muslims' narrowly target their charity is revealed by this question: "What are the conditions for Allah's love, mercy, peace, generosity, and kindness?"

A clue: None of Allah's 99 names include humble, redeemer, God with us, savior, jealous, husband, meek, friend, long-suffering, helpmate, or father.

An Allah that loves conditionally raises a people that reveal His 99 names conditionally. All of Allah's beautiful attributes operate from a self-exalting premise. Allah is only loving to those who worship Him for His greatness, first and foremost. He has no equal. Even if Allah had a son that could save the world from their sin, He would never send him to do so. To yearn for human connection shows weakness. Allah stands above all other Gods for His greatness, not His love. Those who do not worship Him for His greatness justifiably do not receive His mercy, kindness, forgiveness, protection, etc.

Allah makes no sacrifices for an unworthy person. Muslims are true to who they believe their God to be. Water cannot rise above its source. To expect a Muslim to act differently is foolish. "You can't give away what you don't have." (Qur'an 3:32, 3:54, 5:18, 8:30)

Someone always argues, "Christians have committed the same evils as Muslims. Why single out Muslims?"

When Christians do not return kindness for evil, or love the naturally unlovable, they are not obedient to what Jesus clearly taught. Islam supports no such teaching. It does not represent Allah (Matthew 5:38-48).

A worshiper of Allah could not rely on the Allah in the Qur'an to give them the strength to step in front of a bullet meant for a Christian. Nor forgive another Muslim that murdered their family and then help that murderer with their wounds. Allah does not require such anti-deserving kindness because He doesn't possess it.

Jesus' words, "You must be born again," suddenly reveal their critical necessity. Without the selfless nature of God within us, we cannot humbly consider others more important than ourselves. The acid test for Christian love, returning kindness for evil (forgiveness with a gift), is not taught and modeled by Muslims (or any other religion) because only the God of Christianity possesses selfless love. Being foreign to their spiritual values, when Muslims receive kindness for evil from a Christian, they often mistake it for weakness.

Starting to understand why God exalts humility?

....

Now the bloody punches.

Even though many Christians say they believe in a God Who puts others before Himself, they rarely do so themselves. Many who call themselves "Christians" prefers their happiness over their faith.

On one hand, a Muslim will often die for their self-serving Allah on account of His greatness. On the other, many Christians will not surrender their life or even their stuff for God to direct them how to love selflessly. Add to that, the God of Christianity sent His Son to die to redeem them, Allah requires His followers to redeem themselves, and fearfully so. Ouch.

Why backwards? Those who work for their salvation serve their pride. Muslims and Christians alike. They become their own savior. It's self-glorifying.

"Though I give my body up to be burned, but do not have love, it profits me nothing." First Corinthians 13:3

Listed are several off the wall questions:

Suppose a Muslim calls out to God, believing God's name is "Allah," to sincerely obey the Spirit's leading and live out the principles of the Bible? To selflessly love the naturally unlovable. To give to those who hate you and cannot pay you back. To bless those who curse you. To forgive those who deserve punishment. To love those with different beliefs. To live like the sheep in Matthew 25.

If you are Christian, you do not even believe the God of the Qur'an truly exists. And you know that the God you worship loves that praying Muslim and hears their sincere heart. When the Muslim honestly prays to have a heart like Jesus, possibly revealed by the Spirit in a dream, could the God of the Bible humbly overlook their ignorance, "You didn't get My name right, but I know you meant Me." Does He look at their heart and answer their prayer?

Does Yahweh care by what name we call Him, if we worship Who He is? Or suppose we pray, calling Him by His true name, but not in agreement with His heart? Nor want to know His heart? How many who claim Christianity live out agape love?

Is God listening to a person's heart or their words?

If a Muslim asked God to give them His strength, would Jesus, Who died for that Muslim, gladly fill them with His Spirit and enable them to live selflessly? Is Jesus stingy with His Spirit, nature, or wisdom (Luke 11:13)? Even if you get His name wrong?

Like the wind, we do not know where the Holy Spirit comes from or where He is going. And again, how did Jesus respond to those who honestly could not stomach His upside-down teaching? "I forgive them for not believing in Me. But they will not be forgiven for rejecting the Holy Spirit's clear leading in their lives."

Jesus trusted the Holy Spirit to reveal His truths. Are we offended if the Holy Spirit chooses to overlook someone's lack of understanding Christ's cross? Remember, it was Jesus Who asked for His Father to forgive His torturers and mockers. (John 3:7, 8, Mark 3:29,30)

Christ's sacrifice cost Him an extreme measure of pain. Nevertheless, Jesus said the unpardonable sin was rejecting the Holy Spirit's voice, not rejecting Him. Jesus understood there were honest doubters who did not comprehend the nature of His first coming, being the humble Lamb of God. The unpardonable sin constitutes denying that God's Holy Spirit speaks clearly into everyone's heart.

That is intriguing. Rejecting Jesus, He still grants forgiveness. If the Holy Spirit is disobeyed, their sin is unforgiveable because it is committed deliberately, without confusion. But what if just the Holy Spirit is obeyed? Why is the Holy Spirit convicting the world of what's wrong, right, and future judgement, if obeying that conviction lands them in eternity apart from God? Matthew 12:31, Luke 12:10, John 16:8, Acts 7:51

Can a person worship Allah and worship Jesus? Such an arrangement constitutes Allah's unpardonable sin. But how does a humble God answer that question?

Three biblical examples to consider:

Can a person bow to a man-made god and still have God's blessing? How many spiritual hoops must someone jump through to be accepted by God?

Elisha told Naaman, a pagan military commander, to go and wash seven times in the Jordan river and his leprosy would be cleansed. Naaman did. Afterwards Naaman confessed that the God of Israel was the only true God. Then Naaman asked Elisha, "May the Lord pardon me when I bow together with my king, to hold his weak body, to worship in the Temple of Rimmon?" 2 Kings 5:1-19

Elisha answered, "Go in peace." Elisha never required Naaman to quit serving his king, bow down to Yahweh, to bring a sacrifice or say a specific prayer. Or even to be circumcised. Elisha told him to go in peace because he believed in the God of Israel after being healed.

And we all scratch our heads when thinking about the thief on the cross next to Jesus. He believed while watching Who he believed in die a criminal's death. His faith was amazing, but how many doctrinal boxes did he not check off?

The thief confessed, "I am guilty. Jesus is innocent and He has a kingdom not of this world. I want to go there in a few minutes." And to ask, "Remember me when You enter into Your kingdom" indicates the thief believed in Jesus' forgiving heart. He witnessed it.

The thief understood nothing of Christ's redemptive sacrifice to base his forgiveness on for his sins. Nor does Jesus explain to him the Gospel in a nutshell. *What made his faith remarkable was that he believed despite Christ's cross, not because of it.* Yet Jesus answered, "Today you will be with Me in Paradise." The thief knew he had a need beyond his ability and he asked dying Jesus to meet that need without a clue how. Luke 23:40-43

Remember the "lost and found" chapter, Luke 15? Jesus states that the love of the shepherd for his clueless lost lamb, unable to find his way home, sent the shepherd searching. And the preciousness the coin owner placed on his lost but powerless coin to return to the other nine, sent him searching. Neither waited. God's holiness was instantly satisfied, not by their finding their own way back, but by their wanting to come back, proved by humble repentance.

One last provocative thought.

In Hebrews 9:22 we read, "...without the shedding of blood there is no forgiveness." And Leviticus 17:11, "for the life of the creature is in the blood, ...since it is the lifeblood that makes atonement." Throughout the Old Testament the Jews strongly and justifiably believed that blood must be shed for the forgiveness of sins.

Today, as the writer of Hebrews informs us, we know that the blood of bulls and goats never took away our sins. Blood sacrifices only pointed to the substitutionary sacrifice of Christ's blood. Hebrews 10:4

To reveal the depth of His love, God planned before the foundations of the world to sacrifice the life blood of His Son for the remission of our sins. Innocent blood must be shed for the guilty for forgiveness. Even though a shadow of this future truth, God required very elaborate rituals in the sacrificial system. To corrupt those rituals in the smallest manner meant being cut off from Israel or even death. Leviticus 10:2

For God to allow forgiveness, without the shedding of blood, He would violate His highly detailed model of Christ's cross.

However, in Leviticus 4:11, if a poor person could not afford a couple of pigeons (blood offering), they could bring flour to sacrifice for their sins. No blood shed, yet mercy provided forgiveness of sins.

What does God permitting that "bloodless" sacrifice tell us? God's mercy triumphs over poverty. How? God looks at the heart making the sacrifice, not on the sacrifice. What then is the actual sacrifice God expects of us? "The sacrifice pleasing to God is a broken spirit. You will not despise a broken and humble heart." Psalms 51:17

Not until after the cross did the Jews grasp that their long-standing core belief was only a model, not the real thing. They justifiably mistook a shadow for an actuality, holding onto Moses's law, not King David's confession in Psalms 51. Similarly, Samuel tells King Saul, "I desire obedience, not sacrifice." 1 Samuel 15, Matthew 12:7, Hebrews 10:4-10

Today, does God show mercy when someone's heart is broken and obedient to Him even if their understanding of Christ's redemption is misunderstood? Or non-existent?

James claims that even those who call themselves Christians are tried by God's Royal Law. Just one law, created by the King Himself. The highest court, not an insignificant lower court preoccupied with shadows and sins. The Royal Law of love. Agape love, whose Source can only be obedience to Christ. Those who obeyed His Royal law are tried in the "Court of Injustice," because we are judged by God's mercy. A court where His humble love created one ultimate law that decrees that *mercy triumphs over judgement.* James 2:13, 1 John 4:12-18, Matthew 16:27, 25:31-46, John 5:27-29, 1 Corinthians 13, 1 Timothy 1:13

In "God's Courthouse," we will never counsel Him on what justice looks like. We sit peacefully, knowing our family standing is found in God's agape love, both received from Him and then given by us.

We have a false peace if our lives do not walk out the love He worked into our lives. The words we prayed for salvation will not be what God uses as evidence of our salvation. Agape love is our proof. John 3:16, 1 John 3:16-21, 4:17

9

Seek My Face

Challenging Thoughts

When evaluating our own strengths, our pride fools us like envisioning a mirage in the desert.

Before a person becomes an out-of-control gambler, their pride first persuades themselves, "Self-control with money is one of my strong suits. I can stop this anytime I want."

Before a person becomes addicted to porn their pride shrugs, "This is an area I am immune. A little harmless excitement will never control me."

When a spouse enjoys flirting with their co-worker, they assure themself, "There is no way this will lead to anything romantic. I possess the strength to cut my emotions off anytime."

Their strengths, not their weaknesses, are a mirage. Their pride is their deceiving culprit, "No need to pull back and get God's heart on this issue. I am solid here."

As in war, the castle is breached on the side the king thinks he is most secure, placing no warriors there to protect it.

"Therefore, let him who thinks he stands take heed lest he fall" (First Corinthians 10:12).

Story Three

The next morning, with Sergio still asleep, Pastor Denver managed to slide himself into his wheelchair on the wooden transfer board they gave him. He then wheeled himself out to the cafeteria to meet his former assistant pastor for breakfast.

"Hi Bryan, thanks for coming to visit me," Denver greeted as he poured two cups of coffee and asked, "Has it been about five years?"

Bryan cut past the small talk, "About that, but how are you feeling? What did Dr. Rylie say?"

"Well, my body is totally in God's hands. But I have peace about that. What I do not have peace about is us. I am not sure we ended things well."

"We didn't, probably my fault," Bryan admitted. "Ironically, God recently gave me a taste of my own medicine. My new church hired an energetic youth pastor, Jason. And, like you always said, 'Everyone has strengths and everyone has weaknesses.' And, like me, it is his strengths not his weaknesses that cause the biggest problems. He thinks he can do no wrong when relying on his giftedness. He is his own boss and I am clearly in God's way."

"Oh yeah," Pastor Denver smiled, "The ole 'an unguarded strength is a double weakness' trap. So, what did you do?"

"Well, first I wanted to hang him by his toes but before I got the rope God reminded me of my history with you. I was just like him when under your authority. I thought my awesome kindness should never be harnessed. I resisted you because I thought you hindered God's work in me. So, as I am sure you remember all too well, I trusted my strengths, thinking I was God's ringer to the church."

Denver nodded in agreement, "I illustrate an unguarded strength like a protected fortress built on a hill. On one side is the hostile ocean, on another side a sheer cliff and one side a raging river. That leaves only one side exposed for the castle's king to guard against in an attack. But the fortress falls because the enemy strikes where the king remains unguarded. A strength turns into their greatest weakness."

Pastor Denver asked, "Did Jason hear your wisdom?"

"Well, some days better than others. I catch him undermining my authority without him even realizing it. Blows my mind how pride can creep into a person's strengths even when they are doing God's work."

"Pride reveals itself by how convincingly it fights to control instead of calmly yielding to Jesus." Pastor Denver looked at Bryan and asked again, "Before we get in line to grab some breakfast, what about us? Are we good?"

"I will get to that in a second." Bryan continued, "I got a hot tip from God through dealing with Jason I wanted to tell you."

Bryan breathed deeply, then started, "It took me a long time to learn to get over myself, especially my 'incredible' strengths," Pastor Bryan acknowledged as he chuckled at himself. "But, not until Jason came along did I learn the correct motivation behind God's love." Bryan looked into Denver's eyes and slowly stated, "Love is not sacrifice-driven. It must be Jesus-driven. And there is a big difference. Sacrifice-driven love feels like a godly strength but it is just my pride in disguise."

Bryan explained, "I realized the reason I got self-righteous with you was because I thought you didn't spend yourself on others like I did. In the back of my head I reasoned, 'You don't care as much as I do. I win.' I figured people would see my awesome sacrifices and then change their hearts. But they rarely did. They remained takers. But I still felt very proud of myself for the huge sacrifices I made serving others. I thought I was humble when I was really very proud of my spending myself on others."

"Yeah, that was a major head-butt between us. We argued over letting Gil stay on the Praise Team after being caught in an ongoing affair. You wanted to believe your kindness and the worship music would change his heart. And, paying for Sadie's electric bill after we figured out she lost all her money at the casino…for the third month." Denver started to laugh as he recalled, "And when Sheila gave her dicey testimony to the High School youth group dressed like a hooker. You didn't want to say anything to offend her and thought she would attract more boys."

Bryan jokingly corrected Denver, "I only said she kept their attention! And I was right."

Bryan smiled as he shook his head imagining what the boys focused their attention on. "Anyway, what God is teaching me, finally, is that if I am going to share God's love it must be Christ-driven. He wants our love for others to come from oneness with Himself and grow others into oneness with Him. That sequence of oneness is my guide. So how I serve others must encourage oneness with Christ, no matter how kind or sacrificial. If not, I am helping them do the wrong thing. Love can't help someone do the wrong thing, no matter how much they may hate you for not paying their electric bill."

"And, Denver, back to your question." Bryan looked into Denver's eyes and apologized, "I never knew what a pain in the butt I was. Sorry. And now I realize how I took advantage of your patience. Thank you for teaching me by your modeling."

"Thanks, you're forgiven," Pastor Denver heaved a sigh. "But, not so fast about all that. I also need your forgiveness. I needed to do more than model to you that God's love can't help someone do the wrong thing and," Pastor Denver snickered, "how to work alongside someone who you're faking patience with. I remained very annoyed inside. What I taught you was how to be quietly irritated when it came to

Jason. I look back and see that it was my pride that kept you at a distance. I was offended and frustrated because you disrespected my position as senior pastor."

Pastor Denver recalled his own lesson, "I didn't understand it then, but between the two of us, I now realize I took an offense for the wrong person. I mean I should have been offended for Jesus, not me. Think about it. Who you take an offense for reflects who you love first. Who is more important. I should have looked at every offense from Christ's point of view. How was He hurt, if at all?"

"And," Denver went on, "truth be told, I was also operating in my own strengths. I used my own patience to deal with your end-run around my authority which 'nigh unto' killed me. I basically took matters in my own hands."

Like a true pastor that can't shut up, Pastor Denver continued, "If I was 'Jesus humble' in my senior pastor position, I would have gotten the both of us on our knees before Christ, together, to hear what He wanted to say about our strengths. Instead of going to bed at night complaining to my wife about you, I should have gone to you and said, 'Bryan, let's clean up this mess between us and get Christ's opinion on our strengths.' Then, I would have taught you to do the same with Jason, saving you the same frustration I went through."

Bryan applied those words to himself. "Yeah, I get the 'who do you take an offense for' issue. It is easy to take offense when you're in authority. Even now I realize my offended pride is resisting taking Jason to the cross and humbly kneeling together as equals. How many times have I heard you say, 'the ground is level at the foot of the cross?'"

Bryan thought out loud regarding Denver's apology, "Thanks for apologizing. I get it. I need to do the same with Jason. Wow, Denver, I still learn something new every time I talk to you." Bryan smiled as he concluded, "I am amazed at how ridiculously long it takes me to learn anything!"

"You and me both. And, since I am going to meet Jesus any minute, I am going to build my omelet with enough bacon and cheese to choke a moose."

Summary

Our strengths become our weaknesses when trusted. "An unguarded strength is a double weakness." We assume that because our strengths are Biblical and good, they must also be pleasing to God. And, when others profusely thank us, we are convinced we are "God's ringer."

Hence the adage, "If Satan can't get you to stop ministering, he will tempt you to go it alone." We act independently, as though we have no need for making Jesus Lord of our strengths. Luke 10:40-41

Do we get humble before Jesus and hear His opinion? "Jesus, tell me something I don't want to hear?"

We ask Jesus telling questions, like, "Am I helping others do the wrong thing, even if I feel so sacrificial in helping them?" "Am I drawing attention to myself?" "Are others growing in their walk with You?" "Am I insulted by those who injure my pride or do I take an offense for Jesus?" First Corinthians 13:1-7

We can want more of Jesus for someone than they want for themselves, but we cannot give them more of Jesus than they want to receive. Our wanting the things of God for someone does not determine our behavior. Jesus does. He reveals when it is time to give, confront, encourage, wait, etc. Then we will not "cast our pearls before swine" or work in our own strength.

When Jesus does the leading, we use His strength and wisdom. We draw others to Jesus and He receives the credit. When we spend ourselves, we draw others to us, take their praise and feel prideful, or take their criticism and grow frustrated (Proverbs 9:8; Matthew 7:6).

When our authority is challenged while trying to be someone's savior, we find it easy to criticize, not humbly seek God's heart together. Some people need assistance to humble themselves and seek God's face regarding their strengths. Why not offer to quietly ask God together?

"If My people, which are called by My name, will humble themselves and *seek My face…*" 2 Chronicles 7:14

Many are oblivious to the unguarded strength trap because they are led to believe God focuses on their performance, not our obedience. Many then adopted what could be labeled "ant farm" theology.

An ant farm has dirt sandwiched between two clear panels. The ants can be observed as they dig their tunnels, carrying twice their weight while climbing all over each other. The young ant farm owner checks up on them once or twice a day, impressed by their digging new tunnels and rewards the ants with food and water.

Likewise, many Christians think their job is to carry twice their weight, impressing God when He checks up once or twice a day and then thanking Him for the food and water they get at mealtime. It is all about performance. Which in turn, feeds our pride and insults His Spirit of grace (Ephesians 2:8-10).

Another indicator whether we are driven by oneness with Jesus or our own strengths is our response when receiving painful information. When we hear of a woman being sexually assaulted, do we take an offense just for her or go to Jesus to know how His heart grieves for her?

"I have your pain in my heart" reveals oneness between two people. For other's pain not to overwhelm us or misdirect us, we must include a third Person. Jesus. "You before me, but Jesus before you." Then, we seek His face.

Do we consider how Jesus wants to heal her spiritually? How the heart of Christ has suffered for countless years over the man that lives in rebellion? Or, when a couple files for divorce do we take an attitude against one of the partners or do we ask Jesus, "How does this divorce break Your heart?" Who do we take an offense for? Ourselves? The spouse we care most about? Or Jesus? (Psalm 51:4; First Corinthians 4:3-5).

The Bible never directs us to take an offense for another person. Jesus took an offense for His Father when cleansing the Temple. We take an offense for Jesus. Matthew 21:13, Isaiah 56:7

If not offended first and foremost for Jesus, we will respond wrongly and hinder others from growing in oneness with Christ. "Honey, you just need to fire Bryan, not let him treat you with disrespect." Or, "Your husband cheated on you! I will follow that creep home from work and find out who the tramp is, get some incriminating pictures and really nail him to the wall in court." Or, "They swindled you. Get a nasty attorney and make them regret it."

Anger and bitterness are often perpetuated by those trusting in their strengths apart from Christ. Oneness with others, without asking Christ how to love them, will not heal them as God wants to. His way will restore them and make them stronger than before.

10

Tainted Humility

Challenging Thoughts

The process that we grow in humility is no different than how we grow in any attribute of God…we keep our eyes on Christ, not on pursuing the attribute itself. As Charles Spurgeon observed, "I looked at Christ and the dove of peace flew into my heart. I looked at the dove and it flew away." We find and enjoy peace not by chasing after peace itself, but by obeying Jesus. He gives us peace as a result (Hebrews 12:2; Jude 21).

Likewise, as we follow Jesus, we gain His humility because through our obedience we simultaneously adopt His heart for others. If we pursue humility itself, we try to do an "end run" around the Holy Spirit and muster up a fake humble love ourselves. We find ourselves frustrated. "No one appreciates me."

Some Christians childishly attempt humility by trying to play the Father against Jesus to get the answer they want.

They ask Jesus, "Jesus, You choose my attitude towards the Fire Marshal that requires my business to spend thousands of dollars to upgrade our fire sprinklers?" Jesus answers, "Submit."

To get the answer they want, they imagine they can secretly go to the Father for better results. They think only Jesus is humble while the Father sits on high and pushes His weight around. After all, "I am the King's precious child."

"I prefer the privileges of being a special child of the King. He rules above all authority, including those crazies that make up new laws. I will argue, connive, and cheat anyway I can. My Daddy will defend me."

How many pastors have played the "my God outranks the building codes" card when building their church buildings? How many Christians, feeling self-important, bully their way to make money at someone else's expense? Until we realize the Tri-unity are not schizophrenic, but equally humble, we will whine to the Father every time our toes get stepped on.

....

Our pride quietly attempts to corrupt all the attributes of God in our lives. If we worship a God that places His greatness higher than His selfless love, we will also.

The Kingdom of Heaven operates in reverse to the world we walk in. The master is the servant, the first is the last, the least is the greatest, to live we must die, it is better to give than to receive, etc. All of God's counter-intuitive kingdom principles reflect His humility reversing the standard our pride lives by. Our humility greases our obedience to His principles. Our pride puts up a false front to impress ourselves and others, not God. (Matthew 15:19; James 1:14, 3:14-18, 4:1-3).

Again, *"You before me, but Jesus before you."* *Placing Jesus first disallows our pride to rule over our hearts. We yield to Jesus in us, not us in us.*

Some folks proudly call themselves "advocates" for the other's rights, thinking they are doing God's work. Politicians love to protect who they consider the underdogs of society, adamantly defending gay marriage, sex changes, abortion, etc. Is anyone asking Christ how to humbly serve today's "underdogs?" It is His "island" and His people. Serving others goes backwards when done without Christ's direction. Without humbling down, advocates feel noble as their charity enables others to move away from God's best.

Without humility, our self-will taints all the attributes of God. If we are serving others to get something in return, who are we really serving? If we make someone more important than ourselves in hopes of getting noticed or being their hero, we make ourselves important (Romans 14:8; Ephesians 5:22).

As Jesus obeyed His Father, we obey Him. And we do not know what Jesus will say until we ask. Perhaps He may say, "I want you to help your selfish sister pay her bills this month." Or "I want you to stop paying your lazy sister's bills and take her out to lunch to talk about being responsible."

Our humility is often tested. Those tests include others' ungrateful responses, conflicts, and opportunities to take credit. All testing reveals the source of our humility. Us or Jesus.

In seeking Jesus' face, we become "Jesus humble" in our goodness. Right Person, true humility, His outcome (Matthew 11:28, 16:24, 19:21).

Story Four

On the way back to his room from breakfast, Pastor Denver ran into Dr. Rylie making his rounds. "Hey Doc, any chance of me going home today? Not heaven…I mean the home where I pay taxes?"

"I will have to take a look at your vitals first, but you sure sound like your normal self," Dr. Rylie quipped as he entered a new patient's room. Not done talking, Pastor Denver invited himself in as he followed his doctor.

Dr. Rylie approached his patient, an emaciated young man who recently contracted a rare virus in Africa. Dr. Rylie asked him how he was feeling and introduced Denver, "Bronson, this is my pastor, Denver, who is also dealing with health problems."

"Hey Pastor, I have a question for you," Bronson quickly took the opportunity to get something upsetting off his chest. "My fiancée left me for my best friend while I was ministering in Africa. She says the backcountry of Africa is 'no place to raise a family.' I am thinking of confronting them both. My fiancée obviously doesn't trust God and my best friend has no problem stealing my girl while I am serving God. How low is that?"

"Is your question to me, 'How low is that?'"

"No, I mean, what should I say to my fiancée about her half-hearted commitment to Christ and my dirtbag buddy who stole my fiancée?"

"I am sure that almost dying from a nasty virus has made it difficult to get God's perspective on this. Let's slow down and just listen to what He would tell us."

Bronson agreed. After several quiet minutes went by, Bronson broke the silence, "I think I need to thank my fiancée that she didn't marry me and make life miserable for both of us in Africa. And my best friend didn't steal her, she already left me. And, since I thought she was special enough to marry, why wouldn't he? I think I will hope them well and get back to where people need me."

"Works for me," smiled Denver.

Denver continued, "So, my turn to ask you a question. After you listened a minute to God's heart about your friends, you went from giving them a hard spiritual spanking to blessing their relationship. God reversed your heart without them changing anything. So, this is my question. 'When it comes to feeding the hungry people in Africa, have you sat a few minutes and asked God if you're serving them the way He wants?'"

Bronson looked at Denver with a blank stare. "Never thought I needed to. I am obeying the Bible. According to Matthew 25, I give them what the Bible says they need, food and Jesus."

"And you may be all good there but let me share something that happened to me overseas that totally blindsided me," Pastor Denver wheeled his chair a little closer to Bronson. "A few years back my church shipped tons of food into villages hit by a monsoon. I traveled with a group of the most devoted Christians I have ever seen. Nothing scared them. Not bugs, snakes, diseases, guns, hostiles, or anything. But our group ran into trouble transporting our supplies the last few miles inland. We asked another Christian ministry coming out if they would help. They agreed, but when we arrived at the devastated villages, they got weird about claiming credit for all the food. They took pictures covering up our ministry name stamped on the boxes. Some of the group I went in with took offense and had nasty words. Those we fed saw the fighting. Spoiled things for me."

Denver looked at Bronson's facial expression to see if he experienced what he was talking about.

Bronson nodded his head, "Pictures mean bragging rights. Bragging rights lead to more donations at fundraising events. They also put the new pics in the newsletter and emails that asks for more money. The ministry president needs to show growth in distribution to earn his keep."

"Do you work for a group like that?"

"I wonder now that you ask. I think they started all about feeding the hungry and healing the sick to represent Jesus, but now they have big bills to pay, a reputation to maintain, and a fancy website to keep posting new pictures. Sometimes I question whether they have kept their eye on the ball."

"I have another weird question. Do you ever see Muslims or Buddhists or Hindus out feeding starving people?"

"Not where I go. Just Christians and the U.S. military."

"That blows my mind. I mean, I don't expect other religions to do selfless things for others that they are not taught to do. What blows my mind is that of all the selfless things a Christian can choose to do, feeding hungry people in a third world country ranks at the top. Which is why no one else does it. Heck, it almost killed you!"

Continuing with his point, "Yet, even serving others so sacrificially, Christians somehow manage to get their focus off of Jesus and onto recognition to raise more money or simply feel like a hero."

Bronson interjected, "But they reason that more money means more food, which means more people live to hear about Christ. So, focusing on recognition and money makes sense to them to fulfill their Biblical purposes."

"Bronson, I have made a lot of mistakes myself and I have seen a lot of ministries make mistakes. It seems to me, over time, Christians again and again replace serving Jesus with serving a need. They still look like spiritual giants because they are amazingly sacrificial, but often their hearts' focus is on the wrong thing."

Bronson added, "And the ministry turns into a huge machine to get prideful or stressed out about."

Denver looked directly into Bronson's eyes. "And I see an overlap between someone's ministry and their personal life. I mean, if I serve others without getting humble with Jesus first, then I will look super humble on the outside for a few minutes, but soon someone will discover that an obnoxious jerk lives underneath. Maybe my wife, the mechanic, or my doctor. They don't care how wonderfully I treat others if I treat them badly. If I act selfishly toward folks close to me, it begs the question if my pride, not Jesus, is also driving my ministry."

"Oh snap," Bronson smiled as he got Denver's point. "'Obnoxious jerk underneath.' Like I almost died in Africa, but now I want to tear into my fiancée and best friend. But then, when I got Jesus humble, I see them differently."

Denver added, "And now they won't question your love for Jesus and the people overseas because you want to bless them, not tear into them."

Bronson looked suspiciously at Pastor Denver, "Okay Pastor, are you intimating that if I was truly Jesus humble in Africa, I would automatically be Jesus humble here? Messing up here means I am also messing up in Africa?"

"I would not use the word 'automatically.' But I think getting humble with Jesus should rub off on your whole life in time. Just like Jesus cut you lose from a rotten attitude this morning, you will naturally want His freedom everywhere in your life, even where you think you are looking really spiritual."

Bronson reiterated, "So, if someone is truly Jesus humble in ministry, then it follows they will also be Jesus humble everywhere else?"

"My point is that we can't make assumptions about our hearts serving Jesus just because we are sacrificially meeting a need. We trip up because we tend to assume we only need Jesus to overcome a tragedy. But, in our noble sacrifices, our pride often creeps in, and we start dancing on thin ice."

As Denver left Bronson's room he smiled and encouraged him, "Hope you get better quick and stay humble with Jesus."

Summary

Do we find ourselves serving those that fit a certain purpose and "turn into a different person" with those who do not? The questions we must ask ourselves include, "Why do I find it easier to be Jesus humble with certain people? Doesn't everyone possess weaknesses, not just those I feel like serving? Whose interests am I really serving?" (Matthew 23:12, James 2:1-13)

"Nevertheless, I have this against you, that you have left your first love" (Revelation 2:4). "First" doesn't mean earliest. "First" means we placed pleasing Jesus first, above all our other loves. Jesus wants us to love everyone and everything as He directs. Not just those we label as ministry.

When immature in our love, our self-directed goodness will tend to divide people into groups. Those we feel that need our efforts and those who deserve what they have coming. We remain the judge of who gets God's love, instead of going to God and asking Him how He wants us to love each person.

What is happening when a Christian will eagerly minister to the needy that they do not know, yet when they know someone's soft "underbelly," they pull back?

Do we "love" the outsider because they only require a little "love thrown over our heart's fence" and we can move on? Why do we find an acquaintance that we know and see more frequently difficult to love? Is it because meeting their needs promises to cost our hearts far more? We see their weaknesses and consider them beneath us?

If letting people inside our heart's fence often wounds us, that tells us something about the source of our love. We know some will walk away grumbling, "You could have done more." Frequently those we did the most for. If we go to Jesus with that person, He will direct our hearts to only carry the sorrow He feels. Our personal rejection becomes a non-issue.

It is unloving to help someone do the wrong thing, but they will often call us unloving if we do not give them what they want. Are we going to choose Christ over a relationship that demands to be loved on their terms? It all depends on whose heart we aim to please (James 1:5).

Hopefully, when we humbly serve Jesus, people will say, "I am not sure who that was, but I met Jesus today. They took time to determine what was best for me and refused to give me anything different. They are the only one I can trust." Then we become Jesus lovable (Jeremiah 17:5-9; Second Corinthians 11:14; Jude 21).

11

Good Enemy of the Best

Challenging Thoughts

What appalling offense did God harshly judge the church of Corinth for when Paul states, "many of you are weak, sick and dead?" Adultery? Stealing? Fighting? Homosexuality? Incest? Lawsuits? (First Corinthians 11:30)

Nope, none of the nasty nine or the dirty dozen sins that preachers usually get loud about. Those sins did not receive such harsh discipline by God in the prior chapters in First Corinthians.

Their offense constituted neglecting cross-quality love while they celebrated the cross. The rich disregarded the needs of the poor while they took communion to "remember" the love that Jesus spent on His cross.

What likely happened? The Corinthian church put on charitable potlucks to show mercy to the hungry. Their "Love Feast." And after they ate the love feast, they all took communion, the bread and wine, to remember the sacrifice of Christ's cross, as Jesus commanded.

However, Paul states that when the rich got their first, cooking up and laying out the feast, probably on one of their large estates, they ate like gluttons and even got drunk before the poor arrived. They failed to put those less blessed before themselves.

Nonetheless, their blatant offence was then participating in communion. They ate the bread and drank the wine as though they intimately identified with Christ's love that provided the cross. When in truth, they flagrantly neglected their own deprived church family. Instead of honoring the cross, they mocked the cross. (First Corinthians 11:17-34)

One very sobering takeaway: "In Corinth, with all their sins, what offense does God find worthy of the harshest discipline? Giving lip service to cross-quality love while celebrating the cross. Proclaiming, 'Thank you Jesus for Your great gift,' while neglecting the needs of those around you."

We must examine our hearts to see if we obey the selfless love that the bread and wine represents. We do not simply praise Jesus for the cross with our hands lifted high, although that is good. We do not get rid of the nasty nine sins, although that is good. We must consume His sacrificial love as we consume the bread and wine. It becomes us. In turn, we then practice the same.

....

We know we must "put off" doing sinful things, but we rarely realize the new we "put on" embraces obedience to Jesus

Himself, not doing good things. As we get rid of our self-directed badness, we also humbly get rid of our self-directed goodness. We exchange self-directed for Christ- directed, producing His best. (Ephesians 4:22-32)

Christ went to the cross to offer us the ability to "become Him," implanting in us His heart and His power to love others supernaturally. We no longer attempt to imitate His good deeds from our own natural goodness. "Christ in me," not "Christ watching me." Colossians 1:27

A naturally good person attracts no one to Christ because anyone can change from being a mean person into a charitable person. But people must take notice when they witness behavior that can only be explained by a supernatural influence. Examples:

People are captivated by someone whose peace is bulletproof during chaos. Or stunned by someone who cannot be emotionally controlled by the offensive behavior of someone else. Or shocked when someone can hope for things that no one else can. Especially inexplicable is when someone who loves the most unlovable person, truly allowing them inside the fence around their heart. Someone who weeps with those who weep and rejoices with those who rejoice, even if their adversary.

Only after we get humble before Jesus are people forced to take notice. When humble, we obey the counter-intuitive supernatural truths Jesus taught, "It is better to give than to receive," "Bless those who curse you," "The last shall be first," "You must die to live," etc.

Coming openhearted to Jesus, we ask Him, "Who do You want me to spend Your selfless love on today? No one is off limits. And since it is Your love I am spending, nothing is too much to ask. You're paying the bill."

God leads that person to walk out His "not of this world" nature that can only be explained by, "I know who I saw do that, but that wasn't really who did it. I know that knucklehead. He isn't himself anymore."

For those who continue to operate their love independent of God's leading, their self-driven "good" is their greatest distraction from God's "best." They struggle as they exhibit their self-made kindness that brings little or no attention to the heart-changing power of God in them. (James 3:9,10)

We read that in the church of Corinth, God personally stepped in and strongly disciplined those who pretended to spend Jesus' cross-quality love on needy believers. But when disciplining the "nasty nine," Paul told the church leadership to step in. That should cause us to wonder how much more offensive our self-driven goodness is to God.

Jesus said there will be those who performed many wonders in His name, but He did not know them, calling them "children of lawlessness." Meaning "appointing themselves as their own sheriff of goodness." And Paul states we can sell all we have, "throw it over the fence" to the poor, and that heroic sacrifice counts for nothing because it lacks selfless love. And if we follow a great leader instead of Jesus, building a powerful ministry, those works will go up in smoke. Matthew 7:22, 1 Corinthians 3:10-15, 13:1-3

Acting "good" deceives us far easier than acting evil. Evil never gives someone the false "I think I am right with God" feeling like being religiously good can. Evil never fosters moments of false peace like good can. Evil usually gets painful rather quickly while being good creates an arrogant self-righteous feeling for a time. (Matthew 5:20; Romans 10:3, 14:17).

And acting good affords us the option to harbor thoughts that dishonor God as we put on a loving smile. We put on godly appearances, pretending we are now living holy as we stuff our arrogance, bitterness, coveting, anger, and self-pity inside. God sees us as lukewarm. Snow piled on manure. Revelations 3:16 (also, First Corinthians 3:9-16; Titus 3:5).

Nothing fails greater spiritually than our self-driven goodness that puts us into a lukewarm coma. We forfeit His supernatural power produced from being Jesus humble.

Putting our self-efforts at goodness aside, we ask Christ for direction, with no heart of our own in the matter, "Jesus, my cranky boss just got terrible news from their doctor. How do I show my boss Your love?" Or, "Jesus, my heart won't forgive my ex. I need Your heart to pull forgiveness from. Let's get started."

Story Five

On Denver's way back to his room he noticed several plain clothed officers trying to look as inconspicuous as possible. They kept glancing at the room next to his. That could only mean one thing. But why would they take a terrorist to this hospital with all the potential animosity? A bullet wound could be treated almost anywhere.

Wheeling his chair into his room he looked at Sergio and asked, "Hey roomie, how did you sleep?"

"It wasn't the pain that kept me up. It was the war in my soul. I am done doin' hard time on planet earth. I want to inch forward with what we talked about, but I don't know where to begin."

"Great. I love freeing people of ugly stuff. Helping people get through hard times…"

Sergio cut in, "Slow down. I said 'inch' forward. I don't know where to start!"

"Right. Changing our lives starts with Jesus changing our hearts. You gotta humble down with Jesus about the shooting. Don't worry about how the shooters will get their justice. Just ask Jesus what He wants you to learn. Ask Jesus how Sergio can make a difference? Leave a mark?"

Sergio looked bewildered at Denver. "You obviously don't know my history of talking with Jesus. Our last conversation was over 30 years ago, and I used a stack of four-letter words."

"The fact that you're still breathing means Jesus wants to talk. Just ask Jesus, 'So, anything You want to tell me about last night?'"

Sergio laughed out loud, grabbing his leg from the pain. "Me, having a 'come to Jesus meeting'? You are a crazy preacher. I said inch forward. And didn't you just say last night that you can't expect me to forgive because it wasn't in me to begin with?"

"Yep. But you can change that. Get real with God and He will give you His attitudes. Then, you can hear Jesus say stuff you never heard before."

"You're asking for a miracle bigger than walking on water."

"I am only asking you to open up to Jesus, asking Him for His heart in the matter, no matter how crazy He talks to you. If Jesus doesn't drop a thought on your mind, you got nothing to worry about." Wanting to leave Sergio alone to pray, Denver added, "I am going to cruise this place looking for Dr. Rylie. He ditched me earlier. I think he is up to something."

Alone in the room, Sergio awkwardly prayed, "Jesus, do You really got something to say to me? Me? The person who proudly cursed You for all the hell in his life sitting on every barstool in town?"

Sergio recalled many of the people he hurt in his life, justifying all his anger on the priests. Then he thought of the terrorists and their anger to actually kill. Monsters! Then, Sergio spontaneously asked Christ, "How could You love me? After your priest ruined my life, I retaliated with all the hatred I could muster up."

Sergio heard in his head, *"No bad history."* Without warning a vivid picture of Christ's cross entered Sergio's thoughts. Spread out at the bottom of His cross were all the memories of all the people he hurt, all covered with Christ's blood. As he looked closer, he saw the evil of the priests and the terrorists all mixed together with his own evil as if inseparable, all fully covered in the same red blood.

Sergio drew his head back and thought to himself, *Jesus sees everyone's evil the same. Covered. No one worse or more horrific, just covered. Totally covered.* Thoughts swirled though Sergio's mind. *No one's sin can be seen through Jesus' blood. But that seems very unfair. Christ's blood covered their horrific evil no different than all my bad. And even worse, being mixed together it is impossible to try to wash Jesus' blood off their evil without washing it off mine!*

Sergio understood that Jesus' blood forgiving his sin meant Jesus' blood forgiving all sin. He thought about how the unforgiveness in his life destroyed his life. Was he going to add even more hell into his life by not forgiving the terrorists?

Then, once again without warning, the words, *"No option"* popped up in his mind. No option about what? "I don't have the option to wipe Jesus' blood off the terrorists' evil and leave His blood on my evil? Or maybe 'no option' means, just like I really want my evil covered I also really want their evil covered? Or both?"

Feeling overwhelmed, Sergio rubbed his temples to help the blood flow. Then it came to him, "I think I know how to leave a mark. At least while I am here at the hospital."

Just then the door opened with Sergio's and Denver's lunch on a cart. Sergio thanked the server and asked, "Could you grab me the marker on the grease board? I need it for a minute."

"I don't see why not," stated the server as he handed him the marker. Sergio used the backside of a paper to write, "The same blood that covers my evil covers everyone's evil. Terrorists included." Then he signed it, "Sergio, bullet hole, thigh."

Before the server left, Sergio asked if he would tape the paper on the outside of his room door. "I should warn you. There may be a looney pastor who will need your defib paddles after he reads it."

Denver finally made it back after Sergio finished his lunch. Bumping his wheelchair into the door to open it, he read Sergio's note out loud. "The same blood that covers my evil covers everyone's evil. Terrorists included." Then he read the notes that others added to Sergio's paper, "Forgive or suffer like they do. Harry, rm. 233, bullet hole, calf." And, "Allah is great, but can he forgive like that? Sherman, rm. 244, bullet hole, shoulder." And the last note, "Not sure if I can. Thanx for the hope. Bonnie, married 33 years, widow one hour."

Denver looked up at Sergio with a tear in his eye. "I knew Jesus wanted to talk to you. See what you started?"

"Getting Jesus humble kicks butt! I can't explain how Jesus talks, but finally, after 30 years, I am understanding what peace feels like. I thought of a crazy question for you. Just like me, do you think it would be that easy for one of the terrorists to get free?"

"If they got humble before Jesus, definitely. The sad thing about Islam is that Allah cannot forgive for free. There is no cross in Islam. Even Muhammad, their greatest prophet, wasn't sure if he made it into heaven. Allah forgives after Muslims do enough, but no guarantees."

Denver continued, "Since Islam doesn't have Jesus dying to cover our evil, it makes sense that Allah is still angry with all the sin he sees. And why would a Muslim forgive others if they're not forgiven themselves? You know... the living hell unforgiveness brings."

Then Denver grinned at Sergio, "Are you thinking about what you would say if one of the terrorists was still alive?"

"Right now, I have the courage for a simple sign on my door. I am just trying to understand what drives someone to kill like they do."

Pastor Bradley interjected, "I heard some Muslims feel so pressured to please Allah's demands to get into heaven that, to earn His favor, they will kill infidels."

"So does a terrorist hate us? People they don't even know?"

"I don't think so. Again, some see Allah as very hard to please. They are desperately trying to get out of going to hell. When they yelled 'Allah is greater' as they shot you, they really meant 'Allah's greatness is worthy of me killing and being killed to earn his forgiveness.'"

"Wow. So without Christ's blood covering their sins, their fear of Allah's wrath causes them to try to cover their sin using their own blood. I get how that relationship would drive someone hostile."

"Right. Not serving a God who took the first move to lovingly pay for our forgiveness changes everything."

Summary

The issue is not whether a Christian, atheist, or a Muslim can all live charitably in their communities. The issue is their source for their goodness and how that source affects the nature of their goodness. *Since the believer's source of love is selfless, supernatural, and limitless, then they should produce selfless, supernatural, and limitless acts of charity. A love that, without Christ, cannot be produced. (First John 3:16, 4:10-11)*

We need to ask ourselves, "How many people witness God's supernatural love in us?" What will people say at your memorial service? "He let me borrow his truck..." "She took me out to lunch..." "She kept smiling in tough times..."

"They volunteered at the hospital for..." Or, "Only Jesus could love like she loved. She not just helped me after my miscarriage, she felt my pain in her heart. Her love changed the course of my life" (Ephesians 3:17-19; First Thessalonians 3:12).

Do we get humble before Jesus and seize the opportunities that come into our lives to draw others to Christ? Are we on "high alert" for those we meet that secretly live in quiet desperation? Suffering from anger, worry, depression, sickness, rejection, etc. Do we even think to ask Christ how He wants us to help, knowing He will require us to exchange our selfish heart for His selfless heart? Or do we just keep our side of the street clean?

Imagine how God must feel if we only get humble before Jesus when the pain gets so hard for ourselves that we have no other choice but to drop to our knees and cry out for His help? When will we ever hit our knees for someone else and feel their pain (Second Corinthians 5:14; Galatians 5:14)?

Paradoxically, to walk together with exalted Jesus we must humbly "stoop to reach" His level. His humble character empowers us to love others limitlessly, revealing His love to our desperate world. Our pride forfeits our experiencing the beauty of lower heaven, here and now (Matthew 5:44-46, 6:24).

What attracts people to Islam? People love the self-righteous feeling of having earned their place in Allah's heaven. Additionally, Allah never requires his followers to forgive those who do not first earn it. He does not. Although bringing fear instead of peace into their lives, they prefer vengeance to free forgiveness.

Tragically, how many Christians memorize Eph. 2:8,9 and loudly sing about God's amazing grace yet also fail to offer free forgiveness?

Whether a Muslim recognizes Christ's humility in a Christian as a strength or weakness does not dictate our behavior. Jesus decides. Ask Jesus how He wants you to reveal His cross-quality love to the people He puts into your life. Second Corinthians 12:15

With God's love riding on the back of His humility, no one is beyond His reach. If not beyond His reach, then not beyond ours to love.

12

When Broken is Better

Challenging Thoughts

Loving parents tell the children, "You can learn your lesson now the easy way or learn your lesson later the hard way." And God's love corrects, "Better suffer once and learn your lesson now, than suffer repeatedly and for eternity" (Matthew 5:29-30; Hebrews 12:4-12; Revelation 3:19).

God uses pain in other ways, not related to painful deterrents to sin. His love for us gets excited over our baby steps toward Him, but His love continually expects greater maturity in time (Hebrews 10:34; James 1:2-5).

Being easy to please yet hard to satisfy, sometimes God uses pain to urge us to produce more fruit.

God uses pain to prune off our unknown complacencies in our spiritual lives to cause us to rely on Him. How? He may bring exasperating people into our lives to cause us to run to Him for patience. He may cause a series of events to upset the comfortable equilibrium of our financial world, causing us to rely on His unexpected provision. He may allow hostilities towards our religious freedoms to test our complete devotion to Him. He disrupts our status quo to mature us in an area where we were unaware of our immaturity before the disturbance. Jesus let Satan sift Peter like wheat to mature his faith. Luke 22:31, John 15:2

God lovingly treats us like a doctor often administers antibiotics after an operation. The patient does not currently have an infection, but he wisely prevents one from starting.

God may use pain as a preventive medicine, bringing struggles in our lives that cause us to stay close to Him. The trial prepares us to live "more than a conqueror" through an upcoming storm. Romans 8:37

God's hard to satisfy love may go one step further in using pain. This test is about revealing Himself through us to others.

God may bring a hardship into our lives that anyone living without Him would unquestionably get crushed by. He may cause such a crisis that makes it unmistakably evident to all that we are not capable in and of ourselves of getting through it alone. He wants others to witness our dependence on Him and His sustaining grace to an independent world that has no such resource (Hebrews 12:1-5).

And when fighting a Goliath, our inadequacies become obvious. We are reminded why He calls us His "sheep," not wise owls. When over our heads, only God can receive the glory for anything good that comes from us (Second Corinthians 12:7-10).

Is it unloving for God to give us a conflict or distress that we don't deserve, but serves His purposes? Is it unjust for God wanting others to only see Himself in us, not us in us, at our expense?

These are pride generated questions. Humility states, "I will not put any restrictions on how God can spend me. Jesus proved His love by His obedience through incredible pain and suffering. Nothing was fair about Jesus' sufferings. It is an honor for God to consider me to prove my love for Him by also *walking through the fire, with Jesus."* (Hebrews 2:9-10; First Peter 2:19).

……………….

When God upsets our world, for any reason, and the agony seems overwhelming, it requires getting Jesus humble to learn God's lesson. When anguish hits, it is time to have a "come to Jesus meeting" and yell "Why are You picking on me?"

Then, after spending two minutes in front of Christ's cross, ask questions like, "Reveal me to me. Who or what do I put my trust in? What do I love more than You? Do You want someone to witness Your strength in me? Now that You have my attention, what do You want to talk about?" Write down His answers.

When we spend agape love on others, we realize something unique about selfless relationships. *Selfless love naturally picks up others' pain without considering the weight. Do I weigh what Christ asks me to carry? If I do, how does that reflect my love for Him?*

When you love someone and they experience pain, you naturally endure it with them. We recognize oneness when we hear, "I feel awful about my wife's car accident. I think I hurt more than she does, and I wasn't even there." During the crisis, humble love does not argue, "How is this fair? I don't want to go through their pain." (Second Corinthians 1:7; Philippians 3:10).

As our love matures, we realize hardships produce greater oneness with Jesus. "I can't say it's much fun, but if enduring this nonsense represents Jesus to a messed-up world, then I am open to seeing what Jesus can do. Well, it is either that or live miserably because my suffering has no purpose."

In time, our willing hearts are empowered by His love and we find ourselves picking up His burdens for those living in upper hell. The weight is outweighed by the joy that obedience brings. (Matthew 23:37; Colossians 1:24; First Peter 4:13).

....

Have you ever pondered, "Am I so one with Christ's heart that I will take risks to express my love for Him?"

The Roman soldiers forced Simon of Cyrene into service to help Jesus carry His cross. But imagine what a difference it would have made to Jesus if Simon willingly volunteered? Visualize the look of gratefulness in Jesus' eyes, knowing the action came from Simon's heart breaking for Jesus' heart? Simon (and all those present) missed the chance to be the bright light that shined on the darkest day in man's history. "Jesus, I love You more than I love myself."

Will we choose to identify with Christ's pain and offer to help Him carry His cross? He will not force us into service. Will we ever deserve the look of gratefulness in Jesus' eyes that express, "Thank you for sharing My pain?" Love weeps with those who weep. (Mark 15:21)

Broken is better because broken makes our weaknesses inescapably obvious, causing us to humbly rely on God. Broken is better when it reveals Jesus' strengths in us, not us in us. When pain restores humility, pain is our friend because without humility we cannot walk in oneness with Jesus. And, if we truly love Jesus, we will identify with His broken heart for a hurting world. We pick up His burden without challenging Him about fairness or weight (Philippians 3:10; Colossians 1:24; First Peter 4:13).

Story Six

Sergio thought about how the last 24 hours flipped his world upside-down. Just yesterday, all he wanted to do was enjoy the "Navy Seals" movie at the theatre. Ironically, being the victim of a three-minute terror attack brought him the peace that he lost in three minutes, thirty years before.

"You know, Denver, it took going through hell all night for God to slap me out of my angry zombie mode. But even more than that, realizing how Christ's blood totally forgives us in contrast to how Allah makes unending demands for forgiveness, I get how Jesus deserves our love back. I am beginning to realize how I took for granted what it cost God to forgive us."

Pastor Denver agreed. "And I think that God is using the demands of Islam to reveal Himself to the Christians in this country. He is asking, 'Have I spoiled you with My kindness? Do you need to see what Muslims will do out of fear to slap you out of your spiritual zombie mode?'"

"So," Sergio questioned, "I get how Allah and God forgive differently, but what you just said sounds like both Allah and God use pain to motivate obedience? That is kinda scary."

"God desires a relationship with us for our benefit. God loved us first in our evil and proved it by the price He paid. But sadly, we are born takers, not givers. If our appreciation for His humble love doesn't slap the selfish taker attitude out of us, and it rarely does, then He uses pain like a brokenhearted father must discipline his child. His heart grieves for those who refuse His love."

"Allah leans more toward 'Respect my greatness,'" Pastor Denver continued. "Fear keeps most Muslims on Allah's good side. He treats the world, Muslims included more like an unruly orphanage to force into compliance, not His family to spend His heart on, longing for oneness."

Pastor Denver looked at the clock, "I love hearing you talk about your spiritual journey, but I need to give blood.

My body is messed up, but evidently my blood is special." Denver explained, "Earlier today, Dr. Rylie mentioned to me the guy in the next room needs blood immediately and he is my unique blood type. Last night, they couldn't get one of the bullets out. They found a tumor to remove first. That's Dr. Rylie's expertise."

"But that can't be good for your energy or getting better. Are you preaching on Sunday?"

"Yeah, but I think I can manage. The doc said I must stay one more night for observation. Anyway, Sunday is set because God gave me my message last night just before you came."

Sergio knew nothing of Pastor Denver's terminal condition. "Okay, I will see you a little later."

As Denver was giving blood, Dr. Rylie and a nurse wheeled the wounded terrorist in his hospital bed down the hall to the surgery room. To hide his identity, his whole body was covered but his eyes. The hospital guardedly changed the name on his chart to "Mr. Tyson." As Dr. Rylie wheeled Mr. Tyson past Sergio's room, he stopped and pointed at Sergio's door. Tyson read everyone's statements. Then, laying his head back he commented, "I have killed since I was sixteen. Allah is great."

Dr. Rylie performed the three-hour surgery on Tyson as if he was his own son. After the anesthetic wore off Dr. Rylie informed him, "We successfully removed the bullet and the tumor. We had to give you a great deal of blood or you would be dead. Your blood type is rare, but fortunately we found a donor in the hospital."

The terrorist's eyes opened wide. He shook his head in disbelief. "I have had troubling dreams. Blood dreams. Almost every night. I keep seeing someone else's blood covering me and I can't wash it off. Now I know what it means."

"Care to thank the man who donated the blood?"

"Is he someone I shot?"

"No. But I am sending him home tomorrow."

"I will write him a note to explain my dream and thank him. Please write this down for me, 'I have been having strange dreams I was covered with blood all over me that I could not wash off. Now I know my dream was your blood that I needed to save my life. Thank you.'"

After Dr. Rylie brought Mr. Tyson back to his room, he entered Pastor Denver's room with the note in hand. "The recipient of your blood asked me to tell you this. 'I have been having strange dreams I was covered with blood all over me that I could not wash off. Now I know my dream was your blood that I needed to save my life. Thank you.'"

Sergio overheard and quickly interrupted, "That's not right. I didn't tell anyone but earlier today God gave me a vision or something. It was Jesus' blood covering everyone's evil at the foot of the cross. All our evil was mixed together. Even the priest's and the terrorist's evil were covered. Then

Jesus told me, 'No one can wash My blood off someone else's evil.' I think this guy needs to know that in his dream he was not 'covered' with the blood given to him. The only blood that doesn't wash off is Jesus' blood."

"Maybe you need to write that in a note. He is a private guy but I can take him a note," Dr. Rylie offered.

"Definitely," Sergio agreed, picking up a pen and paper. He wrote, "I overheard your dream. It isn't about my roommate donating blood to you. I had a dream like it just this morning. You said you were 'covered' with blood that you could not wash off. It is about Jesus' blood covering everyone's evil. You have broken the Ten Commandments like me and my priests and the terrorists. We all need forgiveness and Jesus' blood covers everyone's evil. We don't have to live in fear of God condemning us and we can also forgive others like God forgives us, even the cruel terrorists. Signed, Sergio, Rm. 334."

Feeling like a well-paid carrier pigeon, Dr. Rylie read the note to Mr. Tyson. Tyson nodded in agreement, "He is right. I was covered and I could not wash it off. But do you understand how Jesus' blood covers my evil?"

"I do, but the man who gave you blood can explain it better. He knew who you were before he donated his blood. He figured out you were alive by all the plain clothes cops. Want to hear from him?"

"The man who gave me blood knew that I was the terrorist who tried to kill the man in the room with him?"

"Yes. He is also my pastor. He has about three months to live."

"Why did he give me blood?"

"Ask him yourself."

"If I want to in the morning, I will. Thank you, doctor."

That night Mr. Tyson's mind could not stop spinning, trying to put together the pieces of what he learned that day. *"Allah wants me to kill my infidel neighbor. Jesus wants them to forgive their killer. Obviously, Allah doesn't forgive like Jesus forgives. Allah requires everyone to pay for their evil. Even death is not too much of Allah to ask. But Jesus covers everyone's evil with His blood that doesn't wash off, so He can love us now. But look at the way infidels live. So immoral. But maybe not these infidels?"*

Finally, as Tyson was falling asleep, he dared to ask himself the question he feared to know the answer to, "But who is giving me these blood dreams?"

The next morning, after another blood dream, Tyson called Room 334. He abruptly ordered, "I demand you to tell Jesus to stop giving me blood dreams. Pray to Him to leave me alone."

To avoid waking up Sergio, Pastor Denver whispered, "Your Qur'an says that Jesus is the only person ever born sinless. That is why it must be His blood that covers you. Without His innocent blood covering you, God cannot see you as holy."

Tyson immediately hung up the phone. "Somebody is dead wrong about forgiveness. But why am I killing people who possess a love greater than Allah's love?"

Summary

When Paul prayed three times for God to take away his "thorn in the flesh," God answered, "My strength is made perfect in weakness." Paul's painful thorn kept him humbly dependent on God, not on his strengths. If Paul needed a painful thorn to keep him from becoming prideful, not because he was prideful, are we any different?

Did Paul begrudge God of his thorn that kept him from becoming prideful? It probably was not easy, but no. Paul's answer, "Therefore most gladly I will rather boast in my infirmities, that the power of Christ my rest upon me…For when I am weak, then I am strong." Paul knew the weaknesses that God allowed in his life caused others to say, "Paul is too weak in himself to do such things. God must be working through that scrawny dude" (Second Corinthians 12:1-11).

Pain is inevitable. But we have a choice about how we endure it. Hate it or ask God what He wants. Before pain hits, we better resolve this question, "Would I prefer living pain-free but prideful in my strengths, or endure pain and humble in my obedience?" Or "If pain fosters greater oneness with Christ, does that by itself make it worth it to me?" (First Corinthians 3:9-15).

When God blesses our obedience, the Bible typically calls the blessing a "gift." We recognize we are humbly walking out what God has miraculously worked in. We did nothing of ourselves to earn the blessing and must give Him full credit, hence, our reward is a gift.

By contrast, when we experience pain because of our deliberate rebellion, we earned it. We labor when we push Him out of our way and strive to do our own thing. The Bible naturally calls the pain we reap from rebellion a "wage" because we worked our plan to make it happen. What makes the road to heaven "narrow" and "few who find it" is our "I got this" pride (Matthew 7:13-14; Romans 5:15, 6:23).

Pastor Denver could have argued, "Donate my blood to save a terrorist? He is a dirt-bag who deserves to die. And it will weaken my body even more. It is unfair. Why should good help evil?" But in giving his blood he revealed a power only Jesus can give. Pastor Denver stepped up and helped Jesus carry His cross, revealing His quality of love to a Muslim.

Does Christ's blood really cover everyone's evil? Yes. Even those who do not accept His forgiveness? Absolutely. (John 3:17; Romans 3:29-30, 10:12-15; Second Corinthians 5:17-19; First Timothy 2:2; Titus 2:11; Second Peter 2:1, 3:9).

Being the only begotten Son of God, Christ is infinite and His blood covers an infinite number of sins. Being born of a virgin, He stood in our stead as the sinless Son of Man. God offers forgiveness to all and wants all to come to live in harmony with Him. Only those who humbly admit they cannot earn forgiveness will. God did for us what we could not do for ourselves. Pride refuses to concede, "I have a need beyond my ability." Man's foolish pride rejects the greatest act of love in history because only humility can receive it, then give it (Jeremiah 13:23; John 3:3).

Someone may ask, "If all sins are forgiven by the cross, then what exactly separates a Christian from a non-Christian?" Answer, the sin of unbelief. (Hebrews 3:19) "Paid in full" (Romans 11:20).

Can we wash Christ's blood off others' sins as if their sin was too offensive for Him to die for? No. And our unforgiving attitudes toward those who hurt us only harms our walk with God. It begs the question whether we humbly received His forgiveness for free? If we did, we would humbly re-gift it to those who, like ourselves, could never earn forgiveness from Christ (Matthew 18:22-35).

....

A reason why Americans earned the name, "infidels."

A democratic government establishes laws "by the people," not "by their God." In addition, if the people of that country serve a God that desires willful obedience, not coerced, even the moral citizens that love their God support the liberty that gives their fellow citizens the choice to live morally or immorally. Their God does.

To many Muslims, laws permitting evil condones evil, consequently, the "great Satan." Contrariwise, most Muslim countries govern enforcing Allah's laws, not "by the people." Submission, not freedom of choice, remains paramount to proper worship and reverence due to Allah.

Because their Gods differ, Christians and Muslims define greatness differently. Christians value a love that inspires a husband to risk his life to save his wife from a knife attack. A coward of a man would run. An honorable man would defend his wife. The Trinity did that out of love for mankind.

Muslim men may take the same risk for their wives, but they do not worship a God who would do the same for them. Their standard for greatness is based on His ninety-nine names, but none of those names reveal a sacrificial love that makes Him vulnerable to the welfare of those His loves. Allah never puts an unholy world before Himself. (Second Corinthians 1:24)

It is easy to understand how a Muslim finds Christianity a "weak God" religion. What Creator would ever become a baby to save a world full of hostility towards Him? The answer: God's holiness possesses an agape love that does not seek its own. His humble love sent His Son into the world to make us holy. In our willful obedience, we purify our love back by yielding to His agape love within us, not to earn His love.

Christians must be careful when judging Muslims concept of how Allah loves. Before the cross, Jesus' disciples thought it beneath their Messiah to allow children or foreign women to come to Him for any reason. James and John wanted to call down fire from heaven on a Samaritan town that disrespected Jesus. Luke 9:54. James 1:20

Their idea of greatness also excluded humble love. The disciple's image of God never envisioned a God that would get on the floor to hold His child when they throw a tantrum or skin their knee, let alone die for defiant children. Their God would hang Judas by his feet, not wash his feet. Matthew 19:14, Romans 5:8

13

Are You Lovable?

Challenging Thoughts

By God's standards, how lovable are you? Do you even know what makes you lovable to God?

We get very excited about our heavenly Father loving us as His precious children, but how excited does God get about how lovable we have made ourselves to Him? A parent loves their child simply for being their child, even when unruly or withdrawn, but what credit is that to the beloved child?

We are passionate about the fact that God is our personal Father Who truly loves us unconditionally and longs for an intimate "marriage" relationship with us. And we should be backflip grateful. But is there not a flipside to this amazing truth? Do we recognize that our heavenly Father owns a heart that we can bring pain or pleasure to? That we can break as well as bring delight to His heart (Matthew 15:28; Luke 7:9)?

Some assume that being loved by God means He will keep low expectations on His children. Others feel they hit the peak of maturity, doing God a big favor, when believing God loves them. "With the hell I have been through and dealt out, believing God loves me unconditionally is hard enough. Loving Him back selflessly sounds unreasonable."

Some quote, "If we are faithless, He remains faithful." What is He faithful to? Us in our disobedience and apathy, or to His desire for oneness at any cost? Clearly, He is faithful to Himself and He does not overlook our behavior. "If we deny Him, He also will deny us" (Second Timothy 2:12-13).

Have we ever asked ourselves, "What did I do this week that makes me lovable to the heart of God?" Or better still, ask God what He thinks, "What do You find as the most lovable quality in Your kids? My life?"

The answer to what He finds most lovable in us is more self-evident than you may realize. He loves seeing Himself in us, walking out His humble love. Dust and Deity made one. John 17

....

We all know people who do very wonderful things, but we never really give them much credit for it. Something does not feel right about their sincerity. What is the missing factor?

Maybe we know a generous giver, but they want little to do with the people they give to. Or a person who sacrificially gives of their time but gives the impression it is costing them a great deal and so they set up "boundaries." Or someone who prays for a person in their desperate time of need, but never offers to help or call later to learn how things turned out. What is missing? Humility driving their love.

Without humility all their kindness is given from an unspoken uppity position. The vibe put off feels like, "You are lucky to have me to rescue you." Pride cannot resist having a superior attitude. They impatiently state, "Just get to the bottom line," because they only want to know how they can heroically solve the problem and move on.

Humility freely becomes one at heart because humility meets a needy person on level ground.

Our heavenly Father does not "give and go." He truly cares for us. His humility empowers Him to eagerly pay the costs of personally caring for and meeting us on our level. He weeps and rejoices with us, as if us. God requires humility of us to walk in oneness with Him. Humility is the essential ingredient that makes all our goodness lovable to God.

Only when we walk in His humility are we capable of truly sharing other's griefs and blessings. To wash their feet ourselves, not pay someone else to. To eat the meager food they offer to us. To listen for the purpose of being their friend, not their valiant rescuer.

Knowing that our adopting Christ's humility makes or breaks our spiritual lovability to Christ, it causes us to ask difficult questions. How much does it matter to us if Jesus finds us lovable? Does our relationship begin and end with us being loved? Do we want to make His heart well up with joy for our taking on His family likeness, or are we satisfied with the show of helping others but keeping our hearts at a safe distance? 1 John 4:20

Story Seven

To test the strength of his wounded leg, Sergio stood up using his walker. "I have seen many doctors. Dr. Rylie is one of the best," Sergio commented to Pastor Denver, surprised at how fast his leg was healing.

"The best in what way?"

"I have had many skilled doctors that I respected. Some are obviously very knowledgeable of the newest techniques and medications. But some of the best doctors have poor bedside manners. Dr. Rylie is the whole package."

"If you had to choose, which would you rather have in a doctor, skills or bedside manners?"

"Skills gets me healed physically. I can handle the inconsiderate attitude."

"Which do you think God wants from us?"

Sergio gave Pastor Denver an incredulous look, "I just wanted to go to the bathroom, not go to church. I suppose you want to take an offering too?"

Pastor Denver chuckled, "Sorry. You got me thinking about something that I regret about my ministry."

Curious, Sergio painfully stood still to listen as Denver continued, "I put on an impressive show with my sermons, long workweeks, leadership skills, and building projects. My church respected me, trusted me, honored me, and thanked me. I thought I was the most loved pastor ever by God and others. But one day I got a hollow feeling in my gut about how shallow I truly felt for people. I addressed problems, not people."

"I asked myself if I really shared their heartbreaks and blessings with them. Did I really care for the hurting person going through the divorce or cancer, and not just treat them as a challenge or a project?"

Sergio interrupted, "I am guessing God showed you that you had great expertise in curing people but not so much bedside manners?"

"In hindsight, I think what God wanted wasn't to change what I did, but the way my heart connected to people. Without realizing it, my pride kept an invisible fence between me and those I helped. My heart only went so far, then stopped before really sympathizing with others. It never even occurred to me to become truly concerned in their lives beyond curing their current painful issue."

Sergio remembered Denver telling him that he didn't have God's forgiveness in him to give to someone else. To show he was still listening as he shuffled to the bathroom, he questioned, "So, it wasn't 'in you' as you say?"

"But it was. But my pride played me like a fiddle. In my pride I was able to look great by helping all kinds of people, no matter how needy, but I always had to cut and run like I was too busy to truly get into their lives. God is showing me that it is Him in me that gives me His genuine love."

Sergio countered, "But how could God expect one person to get close to hundreds or thousands of people? No one has that much to give. Even Jesus only took on twelve men."

"You're right about our natural limits. I get how that is in the mix, but I think I avoided God's quality of oneness because I lacked something spiritually essential in my life. If I showed real interest in people's lives, I would feel obligated to get involved. Personal struggles start to pull on your heartstrings. I didn't want to spend that much love."

"So basically, you made excuses not to love people past the point of a quick fix, which you perfected because you gave great advice. But if I don't get to the bathroom right now, I will create another problem that will take more than your genius to clean up."

With Sergio in the bathroom, Denver reviewed out loud with God, "My whole ministry is to encourage people to walk in oneness with You. You want people to see You in me and then they personally want what they see. But the way I loved others, I made You out to be a quick fix, 'got to go' kind of God. A clever God, but not a caring God who shares the struggles and blessings in our lives with us. I misrepresented Your character in a big way. I never slowed down to concern myself for the person themselves because it was far too costly on my selfishness."

The main point of Sunday's message occurred to Pastor Denver. "I want people to know that Your love walks through the fire with us yet I made my love more about getting people through the fire without me. I don't know how many heartbeats I have left, but I pray You give me time to make some changes."

Then Denver asked God a question, "What must change in me to make myself truly concerned for others? To experience what they experience? To allow people in my heart deep enough to weep for them? The cost scares me."

God's answer came quick, "Spend Me."

Summary

Just hours before Jesus' cross, Jesus stated to His Father, "I have declared to them Your name, and will declare it" (John 17:26). *Jesus declared His Father's name, Who He is, by revealing His nature, before the cross and on His cross.*

If we are wanting to make Jesus known, we must also walk in His and His Father's humility. Jesus is the one dying for the sin and shame of the world, yet He thinks about other's needs. The thief, Pilate, Peter, His mother, forgiving the soldiers, healing the soldier's ear, the entire world.

Tragically, our pride finds a way to water down our oneness with Him by substituting solving others' problems without humbly loving them personally as God loves them. Consequently, many of our "loving" relationships enjoy a shallow quality of oneness that anyone without Christ can experience.

We effortlessly throw kindness and clever advice over the top of the invisible fence that guards our hearts. We still hear their cries for help, but instead of "weeping with those who weep," we throw over even more, hoping to stop the noise without sharing their pain.

First, we must slow down and allow His Spirit to lead us. Then we can rely on His love overflowing in us to identify with the broken hearts of others. Without Christ, our self-driven love drains our own hearts dry. (Second Corinthians 6:6; Ephesians 3:19, 5:2, 25; First Peter 1:22).

After spending His agape love for the "least of these," we realize our relationships lived in spiritual poverty. Satan must savor every minute as he witnesses believers substituting God's true oneness for a stingy love that keeps an invisible fence up, causing spiritual twoness.

Why would Satan devote his efforts to tempt us to commit evil behavior to divide us from God when we unwittingly neglect what God yearns most for us, an open-hearted oneness with Himself and others?

The spiritual mechanics of "spend Me" start as a slow drip then increase to a flow.

We intentionally yield to Christ in us, not to us in us. Through prayer and His Word, our following His nature and direction grows to become our first nature. On the other side of our continual obedience, His humble love will become who we naturally are. In time, we become so united with Christ we unconsciously spend Him on others. Jesus calls it "remaining in My love." John 15:1-17

"Do I love you? I have become you!" (John 7:38).

We then recognize that anyone we meet, no matter how evil or lost, can grow into a powerful love relationship with God that matches our own. Now we find ourselves walking on level ground with others, believing for their transformation as sure as we know of our own (Luke 5:32; John 1:12, 3:16-17; First Timothy 1:15, 2:1).

What does Jesus find lovable about us? Do we love others with His humble love, or solve their problems and move on before caring for them becomes too costly on our hearts?

14

Insulting Excuses

Challenging Thoughts

Why haven't Christians set the world on fire as in the book of Acts? Many would answer, "Because the love of God is not burning within our hearts."

What is stopping Christians from pressing into the heart of God until He discloses the overwhelming glory of His humble love for us? Nothing. Consequently, the glaring concern, "Do Christians prefer a shallow understanding of Christ's cross-quality love?" Why would they?

The more one knows of God's love, the more they are obligated to spend. Knowing God's love becomes a double-edged sword.

A self-absorbed husband loves his wife much like he loves his work truck. He enjoys the fact that his truck has no feelings, he simply wants the truck to do what serves him. He wisely maintains his truck to work better and longer. Likewise, a self-absorbed husband treats his wife in the same manner as his truck because his heart is consumed with his world, not hers. He tolerates his wife's feelings as necessary "maintenance" that he hopes in turn will make her work better and longer.

Will his wife take offense for being treated like an object? That is just it. Not if she shares the same self-consumed attitude toward her husband.

A wife who also wants to keep her heart detached and indulge in her private interests, without feeling like a scoundrel for it, wants a selfish husband who treats her a little like his truck. *Turnabout is fair play.* She gets what she wants from her husband and goes through the motions of giving him what he wants. Since neither truly love each other above themselves, there is no violation of oneness in their relationship. Without guilt, she serves herself over him.

Two selfish people want to pair up equally in their selfishness. They live and sleep guilt-free in their paper-thin oneness.

This low-quality harmony of self-interest shows up in various ways. How often does one spouse with a bad habit also have a spouse excusing themselves to do what they want? A wife may want her husband to quit his selfish behavior, but if he does, she realizes that to keep the relationship mutually selfless she must also give up what she enjoys at his expense.

To remain stingy with our loving God back, it stands to reason that we will also want to establish the same "turnabout is fair play" with God. But how?

Are you cautious about God revealing the depth of His love to you? If not, then have you ever planned an all-day date with just God? Maybe walking along the beach, hiking a mountain, or in your closet, and asking Him to reveal His love for you. For weeks we plan and anticipate our vacations, why not a one-day retreat, every few months, getting into close quarters with God?

In addition, the ace we hold onto to counterbalance the love of Christ that *we do understand,* constitutes the hell we encounter in life. That is our handy "card to play" that justifies "turnabout is fair play" with God. Consider these options on how the average person might minimize God's humble love:

To the extreme, many fault God for being an egomaniac that mankind must appease. "God selfishly controls us to stroke His massive ego." They assert that God does not pursue us for our benefit. His love is as genuine as a narcissistic. God gives to get more back. No reason to love Him any differently than He loves me.

And quite common, "I feel like God uses me like a lab rat in His vendetta against evil. He treats me like an expendable object in His ageless war against Satan." They believe God stuck us in the crossfire between Him and Satan. They refer to the book of Job to support their reasoning to remain guarded with God's love.

Perhaps the most common contrived fault against God, even among avid church goers, constitutes the accusation that He does a below average job as Father. "God never answered my prayers to save my child's life. I can't know, nor can I imagine God's reason why, but clearly there are times when my desperate prayers mattered little to Him. My disappointment in Him excuses His disappointment in me."

Essentially, "God holds other interest higher than my bleeding-out heart. Tragedies hit my life, I begged, He never rescued me. I find the small sins I harbor a ton less egregious than His poor parenting."

How many Christians, disappointed in their marriage, fault God? "My spouse never fulfilled my needs. I fault God for not warning me, costing me the best years of my life. Consequently, God can't fault me for my compulsive eating, or drinking, or…?"

No scoundrel feelings result because we are treating a "self-seeking" God no differently than He is treating us. Maybe not heartlessly but measured. Like ourselves, He is pursuing His own interests first, sometimes at our expense. So, "turnabout is fair play" and guilt-free.

One thing is for certain for the self-serving. "Don't dive too deeply into the Father's selfless love. It will upset your fabricated equilibrium."

God's love "does not seek its own," but do we really want God to illuminate our minds and hearts to the fullness of this truth? *Does it scare us to ask Jesus to reveal the incredible sacrifice of His selfless love for us?*

Knowing the beauty of God's love will eliminate all our justifications to live for ourselves. Knowing His love will disallow us to keep and enjoy our victimless "not God" thoughts that bounce around in our minds. And understanding will compel us to love those that we find impossible to love in the natural. Whatever our reasons for not being smacked out of our indifference by His love, only one person is to blame for our ignorance (Second Corinthians 5:14).

Although spending His love intimidates us, in our obedience God can and will bless our lives with more of Himself. We will enjoy the chief blessing that truly makes life worth living. We will thrive on enjoying oneness with Him, making our Father's heart burst with pride to exclaim, "That's my lovable child!"

Story Eight

Pastor Denver casually slipped into "Tyson's" hospital room when the undercover officer on duty went for a coffee refill. "Hey Farid, how are you feeling these days?"

Shocked that Denver snuck into his room and knew his real name, Farid questioned, "Are you here to kill me?"

"Why would I kill the guy I just gave blood to?" Denver added with a grin, "I don't want my blood back."

"But you know I shot everyone?"

"Yes, and I know you have been having blood dreams."

"Who are you?"

"You can call me 'Crooked Stick.'"

"What kind of name is 'Crooked Stick'?"

"Well, do you believe Allah can do anything?"

"Yes."

"Can He hit something with a stick, even if the stick is crooked?"

"That's stupid. But yes."

"Well, think of me as that crooked stick that God used to save your life." Not knowing how long he had to talk with Farid, Denver got to the point, "You say 'God is great.' I agree, but I say 'God's love is what makes Him great.' Did you notice how many people have already forgiven you? Does Allah give you that kind of love?"

Farid confidently responded, "Allah loves and forgives. Allah has 99 beautiful names."

"But since you willingly kill for Allah, you must believe the Qur'an teaches He doesn't love me. In fact, you believe all infidels are worthy of death. But my roommate and others want to forgive you, not kill you. So, evidently the people you shot have more love and forgiveness than Allah."

Farid shook his head, then stated strongly, "What Muslims believe can't make sense to an infidel. Your Bible is corrupted."

"But why would anyone make up stuff that is many times harder to obey than Islam? Jesus asks us to show kindness to our enemies. You kill people who have done you no harm. Jesus asks us to freely forgive others who hurt us. Why would anyone put extremely hard words in Jesus' mouth if it meant they had to live up to them?"

Denver looked into Farid's eyes, "Do you understand my question? Where is Allah's greatness in being all-powerful if that greatness isn't strong enough to love someone who is undeserving? Allah is like a big bully on the playground who hurts anyone that doesn't do what he says."

"One of Allah's 99 names is 'perfection.' Something Christians cannot understand."

"Actually, we do. Which explains your blood dreams. You probably know that the Qur'an teaches in Surat 19 that Jesus was the only person ever born sinless. This is true because your blood and my blood and Muhammad's blood are all the same—sinful. Our shedding our sinful blood will never cover our sins. But Jesus' blood, shed on His cross, had to be sinless and acceptable to God to cover everyone's sins. God's holiness is satisfied because your sins are covered and forgiven by Jesus' blood."

Farid sharply interrupted, "Allah has no son. He is alone. Jesus never died on the cross."

"Who Jesus is and what He did we disagree on. We love others differently because we serve two different Gods who love very differently. Jesus loved even the people who hated Him, enough to forgive them while they brutally killed Him. Allah only loves those who serve Him and punishes anyone who doesn't. So, whose love is more powerful? The person with the automatic weapons who shoots unarmed strangers, or the person who forgives the shooter?"

"You are speaking foolishness and I am uncomfortable."

"I am just asking questions for you to think about. Why is it we love others so differently? Why does the Qur'an say Jesus was born sinless and that Jesus was the only person called the Spirit of God with the power to raise the dead? The Bible answers those questions. Is there a verse in the Qur'an that says not to read the Bible?"

"I don't think so."

"If I give you a Bible will you read the sayings of Jesus?"

"No. Like I said, they are corrupted. Only the Qur'an is true."

"If they are corrupted your heart will see the lies as lies and it will only confirm what you already believe as true. But," Pastor Denver pointed out, "if you read, you will learn that God freely loves Farid far more than you love your own children. And just like you loved them as little children, before they could impress you, your heavenly Father loves you without you needing to impress Him. Why be afraid of learning how much God really loves us? As fathers, we know unmerited love."

Farid looked at Pastor Denver without knowing how to answer. Farid had never been taught anything about Christ's teachings in the Bible, but he understood his deep love for his children.

Denver softened his approach, "Because our two Gods love differently, we also have a difference of opinion about what is weak and what is great. I believe someone who loves the anti-deserving is great, not someone who possesses the power to harm the anti-deserving."

"Allah is great. He rightly punishes all who disobey Him. Loving unholy people corrupts his perfect love. Allah loves as love should be. No imperfections."

"Exactly! No imperfections. And that blood that won't wash off in your dreams is the 'holy' blood that enables a holy God to love messed up people like you and me. He sees us as pure. You never need to worry if God will forgive you after you die because He already has with Jesus' pure blood. Now, you can serve Him out of appreciation of what He has done. From your heart, not fear of Him condemning you to hell."

"You are upsetting me. You must leave."

"Okay, but your blood dreams are His way of telling you that you are already forgiven by Christ. He wants you to know that He loves you now as His own son. He wants a friendship with you before you die. That should be great news to a man who wants to please God."

Denver looked into Farid's eyes and softly said, "I read that Ishmael means 'God hears.' He is listening. Before I go, let's ask God to tell us something about His love and quietly listen to His answer."

Although not accustomed to silently listening to God, Farid was a man of prayer and remembered one of Allah's names was "Listener." He accepted Denver's challenge.

God brought Farid's close-knit family to his mind. He thought about how he would die for his son the day he was born and how he wanted his son to know that. The memory brought tears to his eyes. After about five minutes of being silent, Farid spoke with his eyes still closed, "My heart hears, 'Love, not fear, is the greatest power.'" Farid looked up to Denver and with a slight smile in his eyes added, "I am not sure what that means, but I do know I am tired of being hit by a crooked stick."

"Okay Farid, I'm gone," smiled Denver. "I believe you know that God wants a love relationship with you like you want with your own children. You don't want them to obey you because they are afraid of you, but because they know you're a great dad who loves them more than he loves himself. In the same way, we want to serve God because He loves us, not because we fear Him."

Then Pastor Denver ended, "What God told me was, 'The very love He gave both of us to love our families with, we struggle believing He can love us with. And, we can love each other with.' Now that, my friend, is power!"

Summary

Comprehending the depths of God's loving nature threatens our heart's protective fences. God is after more than our throwing gifts over our heart's fence and then we cut and run. He wants our hearts to weep with those who weep and rejoice with those who rejoice, as His does.

Minutes before Jesus resurrected Lazarus from the dead, He wept with Mary and Martha. Why? Not because Lazarus was dead. Jesus felt their heartache, causing their anguish to become His anguish. "I have your pain in my heart." (First Corinthians 10:13; First Peter 5:8-9).

We don't walk a mile in someone else's shoes after they first prove themselves worthy of our tears or joy. If God's heart breaks for them, our hearts break. If God is impressed, we are impressed. In our thinking, we may find their story warrants little or no mercy. Little or no joy. But what does God find?

Nor do we first look at how nasty our past to determine whether to forgive others, "Well, if I want God to forgive me of my cheating on my spouse, I best forgive her for doing the same thing." We forgive others freely, as God forgave us freely. How we measure our history, as faithful or unfaithful, good or evil, is irrelevant.

When fully understood and obeyed, the Father's humble love will produce a believer that will rock the world. As Jesus told His disciples, "I say to you, he who believes in Me, the works that I do he will do also; and greater works than these he will do" (John 14:12). What greater works did His apostles do? No physical miracle that competes with Christ's miracles. Jesus miraculously fed large crowds and healed cities.

What Jesus failed to accomplish was oneness amongst His disciples and followers. Just hours before the cross, they fought over who would serve whom. Nonetheless, fifty days later the apostles answered Jesus' prayer in John 17, they became one. (Matthew 20:21; Acts 2:42-47).

Understanding how God's love rides on the back of His humility must rank as the most disconcerting truth that pride-protecting Christians hear. They may wish they were never told for many reasons:

How can a humble person argue against God's sovereignty? How can a humble person clutch onto something God asks them to give up? How can a humble person refuse to forgive someone else? How can a humble person complain about their rights being violated when treated unfairly or put boundaries up without God's approval? How can a humble person pull back on sharing God's agape love to anyone? Knowing God's humble love prohibits "turnabout is fair play," i.e., no more giving God our snotty attitudes.

Measuring other's neediness or unworthiness is not our responsibility, following the heart of God is. God's humble love never feels like wasted time or money on someone when their response is negative. To a humble person, it was not their time or their money, it was God's and it was spent to please Him.

As Christ took an offense for His Father's House when He cleansed the temple, Christians take an offense for their Father, not themselves, when someone refuses His love. When we place God's humble love between us and those in need, the stooping down attitude is replaced with "my privilege."

"Oh, Jesus just told me how precious you are to Him! Now that changes everything. You went from me passing up a nobody to serving you like you were Jesus Himself." (Colossians 3:23).

....

Tearing down our heart's fences to love others as God directs involves a few areas of growth:

We start with a cursory understanding of God's selfless love for us and His implanting His love within us. Then we must exchange our selfish heart for His newly implanted agape heart. We learn to please His heart above our own and others. "How You want me to love is how I want to love. You choose, not me, not others."

Keeping the first commandment first is often forgotten. Reversing the two greatest commandments destroys both because our motives for loving others changes from God-driven to self-driven. When the commandments are reversed it sounds like, "Even though it harms her, my spouse decides how I need to love her. Not doing what she wants will only create hell for us both." Jesus always pleased His Father first, placing His Father's will above all others, including His own. We must also. (Matthew 21:13, 22:38-39)

Next, we realize with His love within us, we do not spend our own love, removing the old fear of being personally abused and left empty. "You mean I don't need to muster up some warm feelings in me for that bozo? That's a relief. I can't love them. God will have to do His magic in me first." *For this, I have Jesus.*

Over time our hearts practice the "skill" of spending God's love, not our own, on others. His love never runs dry. We no longer feel strained to throw our kindness over the fence and hurry away before things get too costly. It is His kindness and it is never wasted. As His heart is extravagant, so becomes ours.

Finally, after spreading God's love all around our little island, we grow a huge appetite for lower-heaven. We get ravenous for more. Now we hunger for more understanding of His love, to enjoy and share. It no longer scares us to think of how much it may cost our selfishness. *We are ready to bet all we have on agape love and know we will come out ahead. Matthew 13:44-46*

As we lived unconsciously in our selfishness before coming to Christ, in our maturing obedience we will transition to live instinctively in Christ's selflessness. His new kingdom nature will freely flow out of us intuitively. (John 7:38-39, 10:10, 14:16-19; First John 5:20).

"The joy of the Lord is my strength" (Nehemiah 8:10). Whatever brings joy to the heart of Jesus, that is what we have the strength for. Then, when Jesus asks, "Do you love Me?" we confidently answer, "I have become You."

What our heavenly Father finds lovable embraces seeing Himself flowing through His kids. His family likeness breaking down the gates of hell with His love. Dust and Deity made one.

Part Three:
Bones to Chew On

This section reviews in greater detail several of the topics discussed in the previous chapters, with a few new meaty bones thrown in.

15

The Humility Factor

If Jesus never possessed humility, the whole of Christianity never gets off the ground. Without His humble birth and cross, we got nothing. But dressed in His beautiful humility, we are astounded by His love and redeemed. Christ's humility makes all the difference.

What happens if we took the same glorious humility away from His Father? Do we also have nothing if our Heavenly Father is not humble, but everything if He is humble?

If not humble, doesn't that change how He loves us and the kind of love we return to Him? If not humble, would He send His Son, putting mankind before Himself? Don't we rely on His humility when we pray for His mercy? We believe He cares about our personal well-being, even in our living half-hearted towards Him. If not humble, can we expect more anger and less mercy for our lack of obedience on judgement day? And how could agape love be the "greatest of these" and bring Him the highest glory when agape love puts others before yourself? 1 Cor. 13:13

Imagine the Father shaking His head, "You are singing beautifully about My glorious holiness, as you should. But do You know why? Is it that you are thankful that I never lie, steal, and cheat? What do you think purifies My love, enabling Me to love you before Myself? I am perfectly holy, and the 'secret sauce' added to My holiness is humility. My holiness spreads humility on all My attributes, enabling each to reach you. *Now, when singing about My holiness, take humility as seriously as I do. Humbly love others as I love you."*

What changes, knowing the Father's love rides on the back of His humility to stoop down from heaven to meet us in our cesspool of rebellion and indifference?

Knowing the Father's love operates in humility tells us what He finds glory in, which in turn He finds lovable about His Son and us. Since the Father exercises humility throughout His character, and humility represents the nature of the kingdom of heaven, we know that humility did not attach itself to Jesus like bad cold that He suffered through for thirty-three years. *Jesus wore humility as His heavenly badge of honor.*

When humility becomes our badge of honor, our lives are elevated into lower heaven. We enjoy oneness with the Father as Jesus walked in oneness with His Father and glorified His name.

....

As reviewed earlier, God's humility flows like a strong undercurrent throughout the Bible. Let us examine a few more passages:

James 1:5 states, "If any of you lacks wisdom, let him ask of God, who gives to all liberally *and without reproach,* and it will be given to him."

Imagine a decorated Colonel that pursues a friendship with a big-mouth private. The Colonel takes off his stars and medals, and teams up with his obnoxious, unlikely friend. The Colonel offers, "I am the guy you need to help you survive this war. If you want my help, nothing will make me happier."

When the war remains well in-hand, the private scoffs, "Keep your opinions to yourself. I got this old man." When cleaning their weapons together, the private antagonizes the Colonel, "You stay in front of me on the battlefield. I am not sure you can tell what side you are fighting for. Besides, I don't trust you with a pocketknife."

When the fighting gets bloody, the private cries out for help. The Colonel readily protects and guides the private without rubbing his nose in his low rank, inability, or ignorance. Those limitations are expected of a private. The Colonel does not even scold the private for partying the night before.

What requires the greatest humility of the Colonel remains "not reprimanding" the private for his prior insults against His character. When the private acted foolishly on his own, he put himself in harm's way. When he brushed off the Colonel, he not only disrespected his superior, he mocked the Colonel's intentions.

When times are good, how often do we arrogantly respond to God, "I got this." It takes a love peppered with humility for God to overlook our countless foolish rejections of His wisdom, refusing to trust His goodness. In addition, we insult His position as King of the universe.

And when we commit a sin like stealing (or any other sin), we are drawn away by the object we covet. Nonetheless, our greater offence remains putting our trust in the object we covet over God's provision. We slap away the hand of God, once again showing we decided that God's heart is not trustworthy. Our apathy indicates our lack of concern for wounding His exposed heart.

Only a humble God would willingly offer to initiate a relationship with someone that will often regard His gifts as "second best" to their own thinking. Worshipping a rock or stick often outranked God in the Old Testament. Today's idols cost more and are often addictive. (Isaiah 40:18-31)

God gives us the ability to freely war against His leading. Why not just give pigs the power to fly? Could their mess get any worse? Neither pigs nor people can handle the freedom or power. But God wants a two-way companionship with us at great expense to Himself. As Satan tempted Christ in the wilderness, Jesus could force or manipulate or mesmerize us into following Him, but He wants our hearts to truly love Him back for Who He is. Only then can we genuinely love Him and others with His quality of love (John 6:37, 10:4).

Some question why God did not solve our disobedience issue as Allah settled it? Compulsory subjection. "Worship Me as Someone far greater than yourself and all others, or justifiably feel My wrath. No weakling imbecile disrespects Me and gets away with it!"

Hebrews 11:6 sums up God's answer, "And without faith it is impossible to please Him, for whoever would draw near to God must believe that he exists and *that he rewards those who seek Him.*"

First, an aloof, transcendent God, laughs hysterically at the notion that one of His peons might dream of the possibility to "draw near" to Him. Why would He draw close to foolish, powerless, smelly sheep?

Far more telling, why does God give one thought as to what those stinky sheep think about Him? He is God. Their opinions are meaningless. Unless, You humbly care for the sheep, and caring for them means their hearts know peace instead of fear, when coming to You.

Once at peace with our relationship with God, God desires obedience from His children because they worship Him for His open-handed giving, not fear of His open-handed slap. Not that God wants reward driven sheep, but that we proclaim, "I am dumbfounded. God put my heart before Himself, how can I not do the same back? He obviously has my best interest in mind. I am compelled to put Him first." Luke 17:7, 2 Corinthians 5:14

Do we serve God, being wowed at knowing His heart is greater towards us than ours could ever be towards Him? Or do we serve out of fear of punishment? Our reason matters to God because He deeply cares what we think of His heart. We become Who we worship. Do we love others generously? Do we give disproportionately? Or are we takers?

Do we believe God's shovel is bigger than ours? On the front end of our obedience, do we have confidence that He treats us better than we treat Him? Our correct understanding of His nature really, really matters to God. He wants us convinced of His goodness, that He is for us. The person that sees obedience to God as making up for their bad, or trying to pacify an angry heart, insults God. Matthew 10:42, 25:34, Luke 6:38, Romans 2:4

....

Going farther down the same road, "Or do you think that the Scripture says in vain, 'The Spirit who dwells in us yearns jealously'?" (James 4:5). Exodus 34:14, Deuteronomy 4:24

Suppose you have done several generous things to show kindness to a college classmate who always responds rudely. With that history, how eager would you respond if God told you to stick your heart out where they can smash it? "I know you are struggling in chemistry. I can help you with the work that you find difficult. Do you want my help?"

To open one's heart for a genuine friendship with a characteristically rude person only promises to add insult to rejection. If your heart truly wants to create an ongoing friendship with a selfish person, it will cost you far more than offering to throw your help "over the fence" and leaving before being disrespected.

Throwing help over the fence sounds like, "I sometimes study around noon at the outdoor tables. Come, or don't." Giving gifts or time costs almost nothing compared to opening one's heart to feel the offensiveness of their rejection.

God's heart envies, painfully pursuing an ongoing relationship with people who often give their hearts to others and even things (money, food, jobs, pets, etc.). Still, God pursues.

Without understanding God's humble love for us, our hearts will quickly slam on the brakes to protect ourselves from other's pain. "I tried, but one and done. Besides, God made me royalty. Why would I exhaust myself with ungrateful needy people?"

Are we relieved when a needy person does not respond to our kindness? Did we narrowly escape dealing with their draining troubles? With God's humility we put their welfare before our own, regardless of the potential "get lost" or "give me more" that follows (First Corinthians 13:4-8).

....

Let us go to Matthew 25:34, where Jesus credits His Father for being generous to the "sheep" who loved those who could not pay them back, proving their love had no "return address" attached. "Come you blessed of My Father…"

Jesus continues, "Inasmuch as you did it to one of the least of these My brethren, you did it to Me." Jesus' disciples would understand if He warned them, "How you treat My dear mother, that is how you treat Me. So, treat her well if you want My Father's blessing."

Instead, Jesus told His mother, disciples, and the nations, "How you treat the least of all people, that is how you treat Me, so treat them well and My Father will bless you." They naturally would argue, "Are you saying that You value the lowest people on the planet on the same level You value us? We are Your committed disciples and loving family."

To illustrate the Father rewarding our agape love and Jesus' identifying with the "least of these," imagine a company owner gathering his entire workforce together for a meeting. The company owner first warns all his factory laborers, "How you treat my trustworthy managers…that is how you treat me. If you want to get promotions, treat them well." Then, the owner turns toward all his committed managers and states, "How you treat the least able worker, even the one that sweeps the floors…that is how you treat me. *If you want to keep your jobs*, treat them well."

Our "job" hinges on how we treat those that are unable to pay us back. If God judges the *nations* on their love towards the "least of these," how much more the person who confesses Christ as Lord? Matthew 25:32

Jesus so identifies with the needy, broken, and hurting that He feels their pain just as they do. If they are disrespected, so is He. If they are fed, so is He. He receives kindness and the mercy no differently than they do. Only humility agrees to love someone so truly that they share their pain as if them. "I have your pain in my heart."

For the Father to know how many hairs everyone has costs Him nothing. Unless... knowing also means sharing their slightest pain of losing one of them. Then the cost of knowing becomes painfully ridiculous. Our selflessly blessing the least of these hits the bullseye of the heart of God.

Imagine the wound Christ suffers when believers hoard His blessings in their lives. It reflects their stingy heart, breaking His heart. But if they believed the Father's heart blesses with a larger shovel than theirs, they would in turn give generously out of gratitude, not looking down on those who suffer. Luke 17:5-8

Yet imagine the joy He feels when one of His modestly blessed children humbly helps a broken person? He witnesses Himself flowing out of one obedient child and He receives the same affection that the afflicted child feels, as if the child Himself, not to mention the satisfaction of a full stomach.

If we worry about the cost of loving the naturally unlovable, we wrongly think we spend our own love. If we feel some are beneath us to love, we wrongly understand the humility of God's love that we spend.

To strip the Father of His humility is to eliminate agape love from His throne. No fence protects God's caring heart.

....

Still think Jesus is the humble Person in the Trinity? Consider the prospect that when Jesus died on the cross, His Father's love required a greater humility than His Son.

"For God so loved the world that *He gave His only begotten Son"* (John 3:16). Who gave Who?

If a loving father could choose, he would desperately plead that he be tortured and killed, not watch his son tortured and killed. Every terrorist knows that.

Perfectly united to each other, knowing the condition of every hair on His Son's head, the Father intimately experienced everything His Son endured. He felt every whip tear into Jesus' skin as though His own back. The Father withstood every mocking shout. He grieved over witnessing His loved followers, bewildered, and tormented in grief. The Father agonized as His Son's brokenhearted mother was crushed by the agony of seeing her precious Son slowly dying in front of her.

But the Father still "gave." *"He who did not spare His own Son, but delivered Him up for us all, how shall He not with Him also freely give us all things?" Still thinking of watering down God's humility when His enduring the humility of Christ's cross provides the greatest proof of His love towards us in our troubled times? (Romans 8:32)*

Jesus came to accomplish His Father's business. The Father's love for anti-deserving mankind sent Jesus to the cross. When Jesus became overwhelmed in the garden, facing the physical torture and, greater still, the spiritual pain of Divine separation, Jesus obeyed out of love for His Father. "Not as I will, but as You will" (Matthew 26:39).

Paradoxically, it was Jesus' love for His Father that kept Him on the cross while knowing that taking the sin of the world also meant being forsaken by His own Father. Also paradoxically, the Father's desire to restore unity with mankind caused His greatest pain, Divine disunity. Three hours of hell on earth. When putting others before oneself, our heavenly Father and His Son considered no cost too high, the essence of holy (pure) love.

The heartbreak of Divine spiritual separation caused the earth to tremble. Consider the centuries of spiritual rebellion and ingratitude from all of mankind leading up to the afternoon of Jesus' cross. Think of the torment Jesus' Father endured each time He answered "No" to His Son's pleading, "Father, if it is possible, let this cup pass from Me." *If not tremendously humble, how could Jesus' Father take full responsibility for inflicting the guilt of such a thankless world on His Son?*

Calculate in the nature of the Father's love for His Son. The only love the Trinity possesses is selfless. Jesus said of Himself to mankind, "Greater love has no one than this, than to lay down one's life for his friends" (John 15:13). Did not the Father possess the "lay down one's life for His own Son" quality of love? More than we will ever know. Yet the Father watched His Son die, on His orders.

The Father endured His Son's pain, and more. The cross was His plan, determined by His counsel before Adam sinned. "The hands that held Jesus' hands down to be nailed to the cross were the hands of His Father." Our selfishness created the necessity, His selflessness provided the sacrifice. Acts 2:23, 1 Peter 1:20, 2:24, 4:1,2, Hebrews 9:28, Revelations 13:8

Incredibly, Jesus accepted every detail of His Father's mission, knowing His final obedience would force a sharp dagger deeper through His Father's heart than His own. The higher the cost of love, the greater the proof of love. Holy love at its highest.

Just as the noble father of the prodigal son ran out to meet his son walking home, our heavenly Father runs to us when we walk to Him. Humility runs with no regard for authority, power, offense, fairness, etc. His holiness demanded the cross for unity with mankind, causing Divine dis-unity for the Tri-unity. His love, empowered by humility, provided the cross and bore the pain. Our heavenly Father wants the best for those who have and will often cost Him a broken heart in return. After knowing that, it is easy to believe He will "freely give us all things" in our time of need (Romans 8:32).

Jesus sent His disciples out much like His Father sent Him. Jesus warned His disciples that the prideful people in this world would also perceive their humility as weakness and they would be exploited and killed. As we endure the injustices and the heartbreak that our humbly serving prideful people brings, our Father identifies perfectly with us. He, as His Son, experiences vicariously the physical and spiritual torment we experience on His behalf, on an infinite scale. It is mindboggling (Matthew 5:11, 44; John 15:20; First Corinthians 1:28-31).

As the Father could not be prouder of His Son for His obedience to walk in His humble love, He could not be prouder of our obedience to do the same. He wants many children just like His only begotten Son. In His humility, we become "Jesus lovable."

"Bringing many sons to glory…those who are being sanctified are all of one, for which reason He is not ashamed to call them brethren" (Hebrews 2:10-11).

16

Learning Humility

A quick repeat of Charles Spurgeon, "I looked at Christ and the dove of peace flew into my heart. I looked at the dove and it flew away."

We find and enjoy peace not by chasing after peace itself, but by obeying the Holy Spirit. He gives us peace on the other side of our obedience. The process that we grow in humility is no different than how we grow in any attribute of God. We keep our eyes on Christ, not on pursuing the attribute itself. (Hebrews 12:2; Jude 21).

The reason why we keep our eyes on Christ to become like His Father is because They are one and the same in nature.

Which brings us back to the nonsensical belief that we can sometimes to go humble Jesus to plead for His mercy but when we want our rights protected, we boldly stand before the Father Who throws His weight around. Our pride wants to play the "I am a child of King" card whenever disrespected.

Suppose we ask Jesus, "Do You want me to submit to my co-worker who insists I do all the dirty work?" Jesus answers, "Humble down. Work as unto Me." Col. 3:17, 23

However, to get the answer that better suits us, we go to our "understanding parent." "Father, I am Your child. That puts me in Your royal family. I matter more to You than my lazy co-worker. Advocate for me as I rightfully defend myself."

The Trinity remains one at heart. Jesus and His Father cannot give conflicting directions. Our Scripture twisting does not give us the right to put words in our Father's mouth when we do not want to humble down.

....

Back to how we learn humility.

In pursuing oneness with God, we proclaim, "Father, Who You are is who I want to become. You placed no limits on Your love towards me. I will use Your love within me to love others as You direct me."

So far, so good. But now we get specific, "How do You want me to love my cold-hearted …?"

The temptation is to get excited about hearing of Christ's humility and stop, as if knowing means obeying. We must then ask Him how to work His humble love out of our lips and fingertips towards those we find naturally unlovable. To "live up to the light we know."

Formal religion has replaced obedience to the Holy Spirit with mimicking the attributes of God. "I need to serve losers because Jesus did. I will help them even though they are beneath me. I will impress myself and others by taking the high road." (Hebrews 12:1).

Jesus never commands, "You read how I modeled selfless love. Now go, make it happen while I watch." Our obedience is not rule-driven, black ink driven, church driven, self-dependent, clueless, or exasperating. *The Spirit often uses the Word, but we are not verse driven. We are Spirit lead.* Romans 8:1-5, Timothy 1:8-14

....

Some question how long will learning humility take? "Seems tedious, taking countless pauses to ask the Holy Spirit to first reveal our motives and then to wait for His direction."

Jesus uses "flowing" to describe how we mature in oneness with Him. In John 4:10, Jesus described our obedience to Him like flowing "living water." Next, in John 15:4, Jesus likens our obedience to a vine that must stay attached to a branch for the nutrients that bear fruit. Each illustrates how His perfect nature comes from Him in a very natural way and then pours out of ourselves and into the lives of others.

How thirst quenching and fruitful is His "flowing" working out of our lives?

Christ's cross makes us "more than conquerors" against sin and Satan. And, the resurrection did not end in a neck-in-neck horse race, or a tic-tac-toe "cat's game." *Why wouldn't the Spirit of God get a stronger grip on our hearts than our old sin nature had when we obeyed our flesh unconsciously? When walking in the Holy Spirit, agape love "abounds" out of us as our first nature. Romans 8:10,11, 37, 1 John 4:13,14, 5:4, 1 Corinthians 15:58*

Before Jesus, we did not need to stick a note on the dashboard, "Don't forget to serve myself today." As we begin our spiritual walk, exchanging our old selfish heart for His selfless heart, we do need to be reminded, "How can I serve Jesus today." However, in time our yearning for obedience will flow with greater power through us than our old sin nature possessed over us. We can take down the sticky note, "Jesus, how can I spend Your agape love today?" The question already saturates our thoughts.

The longer we yield to Christ's nature flowing through us, the more intimate the oneness we share. Through obedience we experience how much God loves us and in turn make ourselves lovable to Him. He enjoys seeing Himself flowing through us. We enjoy loving others without our pride placing limits on who and how (John 17:3).

How long does that maturing in His love take to turn into "flowing"? *That is like asking two people in love if they grow exhausted as their love matures.*

....

Growing in humility introduces us to God and us to ourselves. No different than growing in any other attribute of God.

When we continually spend ourselves loving others that respond ungratefully, we gain a greater appreciation of God's patience towards us.

Likewise, when we walk in humility to serve those who, in the natural, deserve it the least, His humility becomes real to us, even if in a very small degree.

After our obedience to love the naturally unlovable, we learn who we are apart from Him. To our chagrin, we see our old selves in the very people we once judged as despicable. We realize everyone stands on level ground at the foot of the cross and humility performs the leveling unconsciously. *When our eyes focus on the person of Christ, surrendering our rights feels more like losing who we do not want to be and more like eagerly becoming who we desire to be.*

When first coming to Christ, we naively give our humility high grades. We nobly give a bag of groceries to the homeless woman under the tree. Our charade ends when we ask Jesus, "So Jesus, how do You want me to show Your love to the homeless woman who lives under the tree?" He answers, "Bring a friend, a picnic basket, and hear her story. Then, stay attentive for what comes next."

You finally get introduced to yourself when you walk up with lunch and see her rough features. Will you look past everything natural and see only who God sees?

....

In our obedience we learn the cost difference between generously offering a gift and humbly opening our hearts to rejection. Examine God's sacrifice to mankind—His gift and our unworthiness.

First the gift. Not a pet goat. Not 10,000 angels as servants. Not a personal tropical island. Those gifts would have been cheap. The gift He chose to give, His only Son, ripped open His heart to give. The Father would not give us a gift that cost Him any less than His greatest love because He wanted to prove to us how much we mean to Him.

Second, examine the unworthiness of the world He gave His gift to. Are any of us worthy by our prior obedience or promising potential? By our noble character? Do we possess skills, intelligence, or the ability to pay Him back? The Trinity knew that mankind possessed such extreme evil that God planned on using religious pride, not idolatry or immorality, as His vehicle to shame and kill His Son.

Our Father continues to offer His heart to an entire world that has and will continue to disregard it. Being pure of all selfishness, God's humble love is tested and proven as perfectly holy, able and willing to love us through our rebellion.

If not for humility, God's demanding standard of holiness would have abandoned His creation before Adam and Eve swallowed their first bite.

When we obey God's leading, we begin to understand our gifts cost us much less than opening our hearts. Especially when we find the recipient unworthy. Our sacrifice of energy, time and money are a distance second to the cost of our love being rejected. When carrying His cross, imagine how encouraged Jesus would have been if the crowds, instead of mocking Him, yelled out, "We love You for Your incredible sacrifice for us?"

In day to day living, we know the difference between loaning our car to a loving family member verses an ill-natured person. The person who empties the tank, litters the car, and manufacturers just enough gratitude in hopes of keeping the gifts coming. Is it the car, or is it the person, that makes the sacrifice the most difficult?

We still give to others what God asks, costly or not, to whomever He wants, lovable or not. Nonetheless, when comparing cost versus unworthiness, God is conspicuously glorified when we use the power of His humility to give even a small gift to someone who deserves our revenge. Someone anti-deserving. Our first reward, after we spend God's humble love on the least deserving, embraces better knowing His great love for us. (Matthew 10:42; First Corinthians 13:3).

17

Perfected Love Begets Humility

"Be perfect as your heavenly Father is perfect." What about our Heavenly Father makes Him perfect? How we perceive His perfection matters because we become who we worship. Matthew 5:48

It is self-evident that our perceptions, in general, strongly control our attitudes. Two examples:

Imagine someone on a game show that, if they guessed enough answers right, would win a $100,000. After days of nervously winning and losing, on the last day they miraculously win the entire $100,000 jackpot. Their excitement goes through the roof. Every night they thank God for blessing them.

Conversely, if someone was a guest on a game show with a ten-million-dollar jackpot, also winning and losing big, but at the conclusion only won $100,000, they feel distraught over their enormous loss. In their minds they already spent that ten mil on a beach house and a luxury car. Now, all they have is a measly $100,000. Every night they go to bed sick to their stomach, blaming God.

In our own minds, do we think of humility as a bitter pill we must swallow to pass God's test of obedience? "O.K.

God, I will swallow my pride but only because Jesus swallowed His for me." Do we consider humility the downside of being a Christian, like the downside of owning a car is paying to maintain it?

Our perception of God's humility determines how we go to bed at night. *Do we believe the Trinity takes great pride in Their humility? Do They think of humility as Their oneness restoring attribute, created by the demands of God's pure holiness and the yearning of God's indescribable love? God's holiness purifies His love of all selfishness, producing an agape love that makes 1 Cor. 13 look like child's play. Christ's redemption provides mankind's cleansing and the opportunity for His indwelling.*

Take humility away from the prodigal son's Father and Jesus must edit out the Father looking from far off, His engaging run, the embrace, the party, and most of all, His loving words to the arrogant elder brother. Humility releases God's grace and mercy out of heaven's gates to minister to us when we smelled like a pig pen or reeked with self-righteous pride.

We become who we worship: "Humility put muck boots on Jesus' love that stepped into the mire to rescue me from my rebellion. Time to humble down, slip on my boots and forgive my uncle who devastated my childhood."

Jesus preached many strong words about humility before concluding, "Be perfect as your Father in heaven is perfect." The perfection God takes glory in reverts back to humbly loving the anti-deserving. *"Blessing those who curse you represents Who I am. Witnessing My selfless love pour through you makes My holy heart beat proud. 'Look, a child that I flow out of!'" Matthew 5:44*

What perspective do we take on God's relationship to humility? Is the Father going to the "dentist" when exercising humility? Or does He take great pride in the perfection of His humility? Our perspective effects how we love the "least of these." Are we eager to identify with them as a person, knowing that humble love shocks the universe, or are we obligated to get an unpleasant job done? Either, "I am going to shine the heart of God on these people as God loves each one." Or "Once again, looks like the ugly job landed on me, the only one willing to obey the tough verses."

Afterwards, what does each person hear their God say? "Well done my good and faithful servant." Or, "It's dreadful, but pay your dues."

What is God's true response to the child that swallows humility as a bitter pill? "My own child snubs becoming Who I am."

Either we recognize that God's humility represents His oneness restorer that applies His grace on our rebellion, or a required tax that snobbish love must pay to get an unpleasant job done. If we know humility as His joyful liberator that unites His family to Himself, we will naturally spend all His attributes on the "least of these." And every night we thank God for richly blessing us. Matthew 25:45

....

If our perception of God's character changes, our attitudes and decisions will change spontaneously. Cause and effect. *The easiest way to change your attitude towards humility is to first change your concept of God's heart.*

After we acquiesce to Jesus' unnatural teachings of His kingdom, "It is better to give than receive," and "The first shall be last and the last shall be first," etc., we are prepared to accept the unnatural humility of His Father's kingdom. We understand, "The Father finds glory in His humility, bragging on uniting Himself with those who least deserve it." Matthew 5:45, 1 Corinthians 10:12, 1 Timothy 3:7

Do we realize the Father's humility is our "hero to the rescue" or the "guest of honor" at the party? His love passed through the gates of heaven, carried on the sturdy back of His humility, unashamed to meet us in our place of despair, then love us out of our sin and into oneness with Him. (Revelation 4:11)

Although many find the truth new, humility constitutes the Father's unsung hero that walked His love into our lives. *Knowing that we become the God we worship, does it scare or excite us to make humility our hero that draws us into oneness with God?*

As His humility carries His love to us, to walk alongside us, will we humbly love others in their despair and walk alongside them? Will we take glory in His perfect love flowing through us? (Matthew 6:23; Luke 11:34; John 3:19)

When we recognize that His heart implant in us places His humility in a position of great honor, our heart exchange will also.

Relying on His humility within us, our hearts are free to love the naturally unlovable as though ourselves. *Only humility allows us to put our face on the hurting, as if us.* We judge them as we would want God to judge us. We also know that apart from God in us, given the right circumstances, we can do equally shameful things, or worse. And as we look at them, we see what we looked like when God put us before Himself. Lastly, we love them as we would want someone to love us. Matthew 22:39

When we wear humility as a badge of honor, we realize that our neighbor, being a self-absorbed bozo, makes him the perfect candidate for giving God's agape love a test-drive. No different than how His humble love stooped down to help us and still does.

On the other hand, without His humility, we grind along, judging critically and conjuring up a valid reason to love the unlovable. "Maybe they were abused as kids, or someone just died in their family."

When Jesus taught, "Whoever takes your coat, give him your shirt also," He did not add, "Only if they were raised by wolves or going through a crisis." Loving the unlovable is torturesome without humility. With humility, our "lucky break" to hit the bulls-eye of the heart of God.

....

It follows that as humility liberates God's character in Himself, humility does the same in us.

Spiritually speaking, pride and humility work alike when it comes to enabling us to pursue which nature our hearts prefer. They both work a lot like applying grease on gears. How?

If we desire to live selfishly, our pride will "grease" our self-absorbed wish to grab the biggest piece of pie by arguing, "I deserve to indulge myself as much as the next person." Pride gives us permission to selfishly cheat on our spouse, "Life is slipping by fast. I want to enjoy what pleases me. I am totally worth it."

On the flipside, if we desire to share agape love, humility will grease our desire to serve people that we would otherwise find repulsive. "God ran to embrace me when I smelled like a pig sty. And, even when I act full of myself. How are they any different? I see them as I see myself. Here comes a God hug." (Matthew 5:6, 39-45, Luke 15)

Suppose your obnoxious mother-in-law is coming over Thanksgiving dinner:

First, we "grease up" our agape love by getting God's humble perspective. We ask God what He thinks of her. He finds her so important that He would readily wash her feet as she blabbed her antagonistic opinions. And, as He washed, He would make her feel like it was His honor.

Then, when she comes to dinner, *we put Jesus' humility between us and her.* We hear her talk crazy but it does not affect our selfless love mission. We used to fume, "She is telling me how to run my business when I am the one with the degree in business and it's my blasted business!" That changes to, "How can I humbly show her that she is already loved and appreciated?"

After we grasp that the entire Godhead met us in our dismal place of need, it is not beneath us to do the same for others. Thanksgiving becomes an adventure to give God's humility a test-drive. Christmas is looked forward to as another occasion to smother her in God's humble love until she breaks. "But if your enemy is hungry, feed him. If he is thirsty, give him something to drink. For in do so doing you will be heaping fiery coals on his head." Romans 12:20

Loving your mother-in-law without humility requires setting up boundaries. "She cannot talk about…." The boundaries get broken. Dinner is a disaster. All of God's attributes come to a screeching halt. 1 John 4:20

…………………..

On a side note, humility immensely effects our teachability.

Since spiritual truths run counter-intuitive to our natural thinking, humbling down is required to get our minds into a place to distrust our own perspective. Only then will we learn and trust His. Our pride keeps a "high opinion of our own opinion." Arrogance reasons, "Why else would I have this opinion if I didn't trust it as true?" Yet, do we ever consider how often we change our opinions? Why trust our current opinion any more than the prior one we rejected as incorrect?

Our self-verification causes a teachability impasse. Our minds filter God's truth, not the reverse. We believe our own lies. "Lean not on your own understanding…" Proverbs 3:5,6

Also, when listening to God's Spirit, humility frees us from the war inside our minds. Instead of first quarreling, "But I know I am right," and then surrendering begrudgingly to Jesus, humility starts us off soft-hearted with Jesus, before the "I insist I am right" fight breaks out.

Humility concedes early, "I know I have the power to handcuff my untrustworthy thinking at the threshold of my mind. And I realize that the fight that warred within me, that I madly resented Jesus for, was my pride's doing all along. My pride only weakens by life, breaking down relationships and causing me endless fist-fights in my mind."

....

Spiritual humility and pride are not emotions that one feels. They are attitudes that we choose to live by. Christians choose humility because their God chose humility when loving them in their disobedience to His Spirit.

To gain humility, our focus is not, "How do I direct my strongest emotion towards God?" We yield to the Spirit that directs us how to love. His life-giving emotions follow.

We realize that "being more than a conqueror" is more than clutching onto a verse that we hope will save us in a storm. We rest assured we already are conquerors before the crisis. How? *By spending His love on someone overwhelmed by life, we experienced how His love reaches to folks getting hit by storms, knowing He will also rescue us in our next "hurricane from hell."*

"I get His love for me because I have witnessed His love travel through me. I solved the spiritual riddle. Storms no longer scare me."

....

Growing in humility will cause us to lose our anemic concepts of love. The intimate nature of His selfless love will progressively astound us. Our hearts weep with those who weep, not remain comfortably indifferent to those in need.

Obedience broadens our heart's ability to love God back for Who He really is. How? As we humbly love others, we find humility serves us as a strength, not a weakness. Once again, on the other side of our obedience, we solve the spiritual mystery: in the kingdom of heaven, humility reigns.

....

Jesus self-described Himself one time, "humble," and Jesus is the perfect representation of His Father. It stands to reason that grasping His humility matures our love for God unlike comprehending any other part of Him. Hebrews 1:4

Walking in the Spirit matures our love:

"Jesus must love the 'bottom of the barrel' gang because that is who He kept pointing me to spend Himself on. Knowing that, I don't need to raise myself off of the bottom by improving my skills, trying to be successful, fixing my broken body, making up for my failed marriage and wayward child, and so on. His love that pours out of me circles back to stick to me."

Additionally, "I quit looking for someone to confirm my value. Jesus knows everything that is wrong with me, the whole shebang, but He already did, and even now, walks through the fire with me."

As we mature, we rely on Jesus in others to encourage us in our weaknesses. As they do, they point us to Him, even as we lean on them. When hit by a crisis, we need Jesus with "skin on" to uplift us.

Others support, but only God supplies us with unshakable peace, comfort, direction, hope, etc. God calls Himself "Ezer," or "helpmate" because He does not think it beneath Him to throw our arm over His shoulder and carry our broken-down lives. After many "rescue me" episodes, the spiritual connection we foster with "no skin" Jesus grows more real than the physical connection we needed with others that became our Jesus with "skin on."

Our identifying with Christ's agape love for the "least of these" lands us in the epicenter of God's perfection. His supernatural humility in us turns our selfish love into His selfless love, bringing Him glory. (Micah 6:8)

18

The Slow Death of Pride

You may be wondering, "Why make a big deal of humility? Doesn't dying to oneself and living for Jesus guide someone to obey Christ in the same way that being humble does?"

Fair question. And the answer will solidify the central location that humility plays in the essence of God and our walking in oneness with Him.

The same comparison could be asked of every Biblical exhortation, i.e., obeying the law directs someone to obey Christ. Or putting off the fruits of the flesh and putting on the fruit of the Spirit. Or Jesus' sermon on the mount teaching. Or capturing our thoughts and taking them into the obedience of Christ.

Why humility foremost? Answer: Humility prepares our hearts for obedience where other Biblical instructions feel more like we are being pushed and pulled, often kicking and screaming. Or, stated another way: Humility eats biblical instructions like candy.

Take the earlier question as an example: "Doesn't dying to oneself and living for Jesus guide someone to obey Christ in the same way that being humble does?"

Humility already figures dying to self as a foregone conclusion. And good-riddens! "I held up the 'white flag' a long time ago. I know I am a complete knucklehead and the cause of my ruined relationships. The opportunity to live for Christ makes me excited to serve Someone that rescued me from myself."

Humility approaches dying to self like a favorite dessert. Then, humility considered it an honor to know that Jesus uses us to represent Him. In our obedience, we envision Jesus filled with joy, as if we gave Him a heart-felt present to open.

Humility makes kneading our hard hearts into a soft heart easier. Lacking humility, God chips away at our hard hearts gradually. Hard hearts resist, "I must die to myself in every area of my life? I am okay with giving my time and energy, but giving up my money I find brutally hard." Humility already took the "my" out of "my money" and "my time" and "my reputation."

A humble person confesses, "I am who I am by the grace of God." Humility credits God for everything we possess, breathing included, without first losing a fist fight in our soul. 1 Corinthians 6:20, 15:10

Perhaps a wedding day commitment illustrates the difference clearly:

When the bride and groom imagine their future struggles, they gain confidence knowing they are working on dying to self and living for Christ. That brings them peace, although they know they will face sensitive areas that will still present challenges. Naturally, they feel prewedding jitters.

However, if starting with humble hearts, each spouse begins with a different attitude. They are thrilled they found someone to spend themselves on. "Bring on the 'for better' times and watch me get strong in the 'for worse' times." Humility already puts their spouse's needs above their own, bypassing the "getting over myself" stage.

A humble person keeps a low opinion of their own opinion. Instead of looking to win an argument, they are looking to find God's truth.

"I feel your pain in my heart" creates oneness spontaneously, not dutifully or mechanically. Lacking humility, serving the needs of their spouse in times of trouble feels like an obligation to make sacrifices.

Humility stations our hearts in a place to readily place others before ourselves. In that position, we are prepared to selflessly love as Christ commands us. "You before me, but Jesus before you."

Humility compresses two hearts into one like nothing else can.

....

You may be wondering, "If humility makes obeying God's selfless love considerably easier than all of God's other instructions, then why does He give those directives?"

Answer: Each instruction addresses a different level of spiritual maturity.

Consider the various methods parents may use to teach their different children to obey them, each based on the maturity of the child.

If the child is terribly stubborn, having rebelled many times with many warnings, then the child will receive stronger and more painful discipline that forces them to reconsider their rebellion.

If the child is only moderately stubborn, they need attractive rewards and only somewhat painful discipline as a warning. If the child is often "on the bubble" to obey, they may need just a light warning with an appreciative "candy bar" blessing to encourage obedience.

But if the parents know their child wants to please them over themselves, then they only need to suggest how. The selfless child simply desires harmony and a heartfelt "well done" from their parents. Their child would feel insulted if sternly warned or offered a candy bar as motivation.

The Bible encourages everyone in multiple ways to grow in humbly loving each other, using various tools, according to their level of maturity. The following teaching tools become redundant or unnecessary if already mature in humility.

If a child operated in humility, would their parents need to set up hundreds of laws with attractive self-serving rewards and painful consequences to motivate obedience?

No. A humble person automatically meets the demands of the law. Deuteronomy 28

Or would parents need to caution their humble child, "When you struggle choosing between lying to us or telling us the truth, you must stop and ask yourself, do you really love us?" Humility removes the initial struggle because humility does not feel the need to manipulate to get what it wants. It wants what God wants without two wills fighting in the first place. The "who do I love" war is over and in the history books (Matthew 6:24).

Would the parents need a long grocery list detailing the right and wrong way to treat others and give the old "you reap what you sow" warning speech? Humility breezes through the "put off" and "put on" list (Ephesians 4:25-31).

If their child is humble at heart, would the parents need to make it a household rule that their older children are responsible to look after their younger siblings? To consider their needs as important as their own (Hebrews 10:24)? Etc.

When we first come to Jesus, we are rarely aware of our stealthy pride. We require God's rudimentary tools to slowly grind our pride out of us. Every time we hear God's instructions to obey, our pride gives us the pre-wedding jitters. "I feel like I am climbing up a strenuous mountain while carrying my heavy cross."

Struggling to walk in humility, we go through the internal war of dying to self or any other teaching tool to learn to humbly flow in His nature. Even so, God blesses our obedience, rewarding each step of obedience with more of Himself. It is the slow death of our pride that makes the climb so difficult, not God's demands. "My yoke is easy and My burden is light" (Matthew 11:30)

19

Loving Muslims

Countless Muslims have a deep desire to please God. They claim, "There are far worse things than dying. Not living according to what is true, no matter the cost, that is worse."

Allah has 99 beautiful names, many of which represent a God that cares for His people. Although Allah's names may not include the most personal, vulnerable, or intimate names that are given to the Father, Son and Holy Spirit, many of Allah's names are very endearing.

As some teachers of the Bible have chosen to focus on either God's love or His justice, a teacher of Islam could major on Allah's names that promote love or the names that promote judgement. Some Christian churches use God's love to motivate obedience. Others prefer fear. Sadly, fear and guilt typically prove more effective. Romans 2:4-7

The distinction Muslims strongly assert is that they do not worship a "weak" God, as Jesus is in Christianity. Or Yahweh being a "friend" of Abraham. Etc. Allah must distinguish Himself as above all and would never put His creation before Himself. That constitutes a softness, unbecoming of a God that must manage with a strong hand the affairs of a corrupt and defiant world.

Perhaps the Muslim insistence of a great God, living far above the messy drama of our daily lives, can be correlated to a general of large military. If the general becomes emotionally involved in the lives of his officers and one officer proves incompetent, the "nerves of steel" general must sternly remove him, not letting his emotions cause him to mismanage the war.

Allah possesses no weaknesses; hence He allows no love relationships that would make His heart vulnerable to truly caring for the disobedient or frail. No "weeping with those who weep." Allah's love "throws the good stuff over the fence of His heart." *Letting anyone inside constitutes a breach of absolute control. None of Allah's ninety names is "Father."*

Serving a self-serving God that keeps a "tight ship," one that holds back blessings until His followers have first proven their loyalty, entices a person's pride like a pit bull to a juicy steak. They thrive on proving they can carry their own weight. "Fast from food and water during the entire day for thirty days? No problem." (Ramadan)

Conversely, depending on a Messiah to pay for your salvation reveals a lack of personal strength and commitment. Moreover, to serve a God weak enough to become that dying Messiah is even more disconcerting.

Before Christians judge Muslims on this prideful "self-righteous" issue, they should look into a mirror.

Didn't the self-righteous religious leaders in Jesus' day teach that Yahweh was merciless, vindictive, and unforgiving? Impossible to please. They preferred to emphasis the unsurpassed power of Yahweh, His holiness, His unmatched glory, at the expense of His longsuffering, grace, and mercy. As with Muslims, it served their pride. Jesus loved the Pharisees, but He admonished them for the arrogant hearts. Matthew 23

One wonders how Jesus would be embraced in a Muslim country today. Forgiving the prostitute and tax-collectors, healing lepers, speaking of turning the other cheek. Any different than 2,000 years ago in Jerusalem?

And, pride hits us all. Countless Christians hold onto their personal guilt, working off their worst sins.

Recognizing these hurdles, it reveals how difficult it remains for a Muslim to convert to Christianity. Yet amazingly, when a sincere Muslim, searching after God, meets the Spirit and yields, their conversion becomes Satan's worst nightmare as they become Christ's powerful child. Spiritually they fit into the category, "a hundred of you shall put ten thousand to flight" (Leviticus 26:8).

....

When considering how to talk about Jesus with a Muslim, let us consider how people the world over, not only Muslims, typically make meaningful decisions. As a basic rule, *"People go out the same way they go in."*

If you take a particular job in hopes of making a certain amount of money and it generates that amount, you will keep the job. If the folks you work around are too busy to go to lunch together, that does not bother you. But if you took the job to enjoy the people you work with, not necessarily for the money, the distant relationships would cause you to quit regardless of a large income.

Or, if you are looking for an honest person to start a romantic relationship with and then learn that the person you are seeing is manipulative and deceptive, you will move on regardless of how rich or attractive they are.

How does "people go out the same way they go in" work as a formula when choosing religious beliefs?

If you belong to a particular religion because your family and friends made you feel loved and included, you will stay true to that religious family as long as they continue loving you, even if you learn of disturbing information regarding the truths of your religion.

On the other hand, if you choose a religion because you first researched it and found its truth claims convincing, then you will still align yourself with that belief even if it costs you all your relationships. Or, leave it if confronted with new facts that undermine your beliefs.

A great many choose their belief system based on a strong emotional bond to someone in that faith, not "I objectively examined the truth claims of several different belief systems before making my logical decision." When their emotional bonds weaken, typically their loyalty to their faith will also.

Love and belonging drives most of our decisions because desiring oneness with others embraces God's image in us. This point is illustrated by the cross-over conversion rate after a public theological debate. Anyone jump sides based on, "Oh, I am convinced now. Sorry wife, mom, dad, family, and friends. The truth outweighs all relationships."

In addition to the strong pull of oneness, and for others, although to a lesser degree, mental arguments, God uses several other factors to draw mankind to Him. Each influence can be received or rejected, based on someone's ultimate choice of who they love, self or God.

The most obvious influence constitutes how God woos us to Himself through His creation. We witness His character through the majesty, beauty, and pleasure we receive from creation. We not only have tastebuds; we can enjoy hundreds of flavorful foods. Etc. Romans 1:20, 2:15, 16:26, Acts 17:29, Titus 2:11

In addition, the Holy Spirit reveals to everyone's minds and hearts what is wrong and right, and that we will one day be judged for which we choose. John 16:8

God also uses His written Word to reveal His power and character. 2 Timothy 2:15

As an extremely effective tool, God uses upper-hell emotions like fear, anger, purposelessness, and self-pity. They all painfully expose something is wrong at the core.

God also uses supernatural interventions, often giving visions and dreams. Many Muslims sincerely desire to please God. Consequently, He radically disrupts their religious thinking with visions of Jesus and His love for them. Some Muslims, desperately seeking truths to bring peace and joy into their lives, test Jesus and He answers their prayers with undeniable miracles.

Now let us add to that list one more influence.

Jesus fervently prayed in the garden just before His cross, "I in them [Jesus' followers], and You in Me; that they may be made perfect in one, and that the world may know that You have sent Me, and have loved them as You have loved Me" (John 17:23).

Of all the different means listed that God uses to draw the world into His family, which did Jesus pray for? Mental arguments? Nature? Guilt? Visions? Miracles? Verses? Gifts of the Spirit? None of those. He asked that His followers walk in oneness with Him and reveal His humble heart to a love-starved world. Which would thrill Him most? Which appeals to the nature of God in us?

Oneness embraces mankind's deepest longing. Only Christianity offers Christ's perfect love that the rest of the world longs for. Christians possess a ridiculous "competitive edge" over all other religions, a superior "patent" on God's love. Everyone desires a pure oneness that weeps with those who weep and rejoices with those who rejoice, but only Jesus offers it.

Regarding oneness, according to the hadeeth, Allah states, "Let Us create man in Our image…" Plural. Tough verse to explain for a Muslim.

……………….

When discussing Christianity with a Muslim by appealing to their desire for oneness, we can use a Muslim's own marriage as an example of their preference between power and love. Which do they value most in a relationship?

As an example:

When talking to an engaged Muslim couple, you ask the man, "Would you protect your future bride from an attacker? Even if he had a knife and you might die?" If he answers "Yes," his love resembles the same as Christ. How can he call Jesus' love weak, knowing it requires great courage and love to save his future wife? And why does he possess a sacrificial love for his fiancé when Allah does not express that love for him?

Then ask his bride to be, "Let's say another man walks into your life and he is stronger, taller, and wealthier. He is not afraid of telling people what to do. If he orders you to marry him, would you? Or, would you still choose to marry the man you love and tenderly loves you?" If she answers "I want to love and be loved, not manhandled," she just chose Christ's nature over Allah's nature.

Perhaps one more question, "How do you want your husband's love to operate? Something like, 'If you first treat me right, I will treat you right. If you disappoint me, be sure

I will more than disappoint you." Do they want a self-serving love or selfless love? Where did that desire come from if not from God? If unconditionally loving, why?

Why not throw out a few other thoughts. "Now that you are engaged, don't you find yourselves vulnerable to each other's well-being? Do you share each other's joys and sorrows? And, since your love is truly for your fiancé, are you looking for something in return if you do something nice? Does your love wait for the other to initiate?"

How does your love towards your future spouse or family model Allah's love? If His love is the highest love, why does your love not mimic it to all those you love?

....

Some Muslims will realize the contradictions in their personal relationships, others will hold true to Allah's conditional love, believing any love that makes one vulnerable to another's weakness shows weakness. Keeping their hearts at a distance, they can exercise harsh judgement on their loved ones to remain loyal to their God. Judgment rules over mercy.

For a Muslim that seeks oneness with those they love at great expense to themselves, those questions will challenge them to ponder if they believe power or justice should outrank love in the God they serve. "Mercy triumphs over judgement." James 2:13, Matt. 5:7, 18:28-35

Nonetheless, overcoming pride still presents a huge hurdle. Pride refuses Christ no matter how much supernatural love or how many arguments or miracles are witnessed.

If a Muslim exams Christianity they will learn of several unnatural behaviors that require being born again: Returning kindness for evil. Caring for someone who believes differently. Getting rid of internal ungodly attitudes such as anger, lust, greed, etc. Integrity in thought. Surrendering their goodness to God. Walking humbly. Loving others with Christ's selfless love. Etc.

Christians struggle with the same issues. Even with the presence of the Holy Spirit implanted in them, they often resist exchanging their selfish heart for His selfless heart.

Realizing everyone's need for oneness and the many Muslims with honest doubts, we minister by loving them with the same quality of love that Jesus loves us with and explaining the truths of Christianity to those who truly want answers. The love and wisdom needed requires relying on Christ in us.

Will they choose His selfless love over their pride and judgmental thinking? Or will they resist, not wanting to humble themselves to loving as Christ loved?

That is God's country. Ours remains obedience. *Agape love is never wasted.*

....

Why not share with Muslims they can experience the same oneness with God that they cherish with each other? A love relationship that enjoys perfect peace, not fear of judgement.

The "weak God" argument is readily challenged, "What requires more strength: To love your spouse when they are doing well or to love them when they are unable do nothing back? Or, when they act unlovable?"

Tragically, how many Muslims see agape love in action? And how many Christians grasp Christ's cross-quality love? Of those that do understand, many do not desire to spend it. Bragging is easy, spending is costly.

When Christians do not "donate their blood" to reveal Christ's supernatural love, the Muslim is never challenged to ask why Allah's love creates less oneness than Christ's love? Left unchallenged, their prideful nature fully supports an Allah with harsh judgements, untouchable glory, and "I come to be served, not to serve." As a result, they strive to merit Allah's blessings and treat others the same.

....

As stated, to a Muslim, Allah rightfully represents a strong God, worthy of bowing before five times daily. Allah runs a tight ship, as it should be. To them, Christianity presents a weak, toothless Father that allows His children to get away with far too much.

There is a verse found in the Qur'an that makes for a great starting place to discuss which God deserves our worship. "Let there be no compulsion in religion" (Qur'an 2:256).

In this verse, Allah boasts that He wants His followers to worship Him for His wonderful mercy and goodness. Really? More wonderful compared to Christ? Maybe the Christ that "escaped" going to the cross as presented in the Qur'an, but not the humble Jesus as revealed in the Bible. Or the vulnerable God Who asked Hosea to marry a harlot to identify with His heartbreak, married to an adulterous nation. Etc.

When giving people the option of worshipping who truly loves them with a selfless love that produces oneness, Jesus has no competition. They simply ask themselves, "When has Allah ever placed me before Himself, or grieved and suffered for me, or with me?"

Allah does not possess a love that would consider stooping to our needy level, living as one of us, serving us, or dying for us. Philippians 2:1-10

The Qur'an majors on obedience regardless of someone's heart attitudes. Those who refuse to obey outwardly are justly punished. The nature of selfish love demands, "Worship me. Meet my demands. My glory exalts Me far above you. I could never make you My friends or family. That would reduce Me to your destitute level, which cannot be done."

Jesus majors on obedience driven by our free choice to love Him over all competing loves, not fear of the consequences of upsetting Him. Those who refuse, break His heart. He sadly gives them what they ask for…separation from Him and His goodness.

Many Muslims sincerely want to know God and serve Him with all their lives. To the person who truly wants to bow before God and worship Him, what greater news could they hear? "God looks past my unworthiness and loves me and cares about me personally. His love for me is greater than my love can ever be for Him or anyone else. He truly suffered for me to prove His love, and He did it before I changed my heart to loving Him. He forgives me not based on my goodness, but Christ's cross. No more condemnation, guilt, or fear. In serving Him, I will also love others as He loves, no matter who and what it costs."

Jesus' limitless love empowers their hearts into obeying Him out of appreciation for His great love, not under threat of being rejected.

....

How do Christians explain how God's love does not also make Him a push-over? Weak? How is He capable of managing a hostile world packed full of self-serving idiots? How does a Christian respond to a Muslim's need to believe His God is in control, yet walking with us?

One gentle response would be that God focuses His power to restore us, not punish us, in our disobedience. Much like a parent exercises self-control because they want to teach their rebellious two-year child, not prove to the child who is the boss by forcefully spanking them. If God needed to prove He was in control by punishing disobedience, He stops being in control. Like the lion chuckles at the threats made by a taunting sheep.

Using reality, perhaps causally asking, "You don't want to worship a God that does not run a tight ship? One that proves His power by demanding obedience and punishing disobedience? Have you considered how much Allah is really taking control, or proving His 'greatness' in this world?"

For the Muslim who looks the world over, they must wonder why the most powerful militaries are in non-Muslim countries? Where is Allah's power when a Muslim country is under attack or occupied? Why are non-Muslim countries prospering? Inventing everything? Blessed with majestic mountains, oceans, forests, etc.? On what level are non-Muslim countries punished for not worshipping Allah? Seems Allah isn't in charge of much of the ship.

In addition, Muslims are forced to address what Christians must also address. "Why the heck isn't my all-powerful God doing anything about all the terrible things going on in the world? And in my life?"

Christians do have answers, but all their answers relate to His humble love, not lack of power. Answers like, "This brutal world reveals the depth of His love by the price He was willing to pay for it." And, "God reveals His love by willingly walking "though the fire with us." And, "God gives us a choice to love Him back because He wants our love to be as pure as His." And, "He desires us to understand what pain He endures when we hurt Him." Finally, "He gives us opportunities to minister His love to others."

If in Christianity God seems like a glutton for punishment, His infinite love answers back, "I never give up hope. I find My glory shines the brightest in the sacrifice My humble love willingly pays. Even when spent without anyone taking notice. Much like the gorgeous flowers I placed on mountains that no one will ever see. Agape love is never wasted."

On the other hand, how does Allah answer the same question, "Why don't You do something about this world living in rebellion against You?" Although Allah remains immune from anyone breaking His heart, He demands respect. What happened to His great power? Without selfless love as His explanation, where is His power ruling the day?

Possibly, either Allah has more mercy than He wants to let on, or He is one miserable Almighty God that cannot keep His ship in order. If He does show mercy on the undeserving, then Muslims should follow. Mercy, not justice, on half-hearted Muslims. And mercy, not justice, on infidels.

Ironically, this crazy world gives the "weak" God of the Bible the glory He intended. However, the same rebellion means the "Almighty" God of Islam does not receive the glory He demands. In the end, which one operates in the power they claim to possess? The power of agape love or the power of might?

....

Imagine going from believing, "Allah wants me to serve Him and maybe if I am good enough, He will let me into heaven," to knowing, "The Creator of the Universe truly wants to enjoy a two-way friendship here and now, making peace between us." Love rules, not fear.

Understandably, Muslims often criticize Christians for the typical Christian's shallow commitment to their faith. Frankly, their criticism is not unwarranted. But once the Muslim understands the motivating factors of obedience to Christ and Allah are basically opposed to each other, they should consider withholding critical judgement. For example:

Fear motivates obedience far easier than selfless love. And in Christianity, one's pride must surrender to humility. Christ's selfless love demands far more of one's heart than Allah's selfish love. Like returning kindness for evil. And spending agape love requires putting someone above yourself, a far more demanding sacrifice than giving a gift and then getting far away.

Further, with the Spirit within us, God examines our hearts. Repentance moves from parroting a prayer to the desire to stop breaking a Person's heart. Weeping with those who weep means letting others inside the fence that surrounds your heart, including those who have harmed us. Christians serve whoever Christ directs them to serve, "you before me, but Jesus before you." Etc.

When Muslims realize the Christian faith first requires a selfless heart implant and then a heart exchange, they begin to understand why Jesus stated His was the "narrow road." Growing in oneness with God and others will challenge every "not-God" thought in us. Finally, Christ's cross raises the bar to spending His "cross-quality love."

Our reward constitutes pure oneness.

....

Christians must reveal the humble heart of God to Muslims no differently than to anyone else. Jesus prayed that His followers would reveal His great love to all the world, attracting the world to Him. With the access to the internet, curious Muslims will learn more than their spiritual leaders are telling them about the Bible, Christ, and Christians.

As many Muslims that have converted to following Jesus testify, they found an emptiness in Islam. Many struggle with the common hatred of others. And many fear dying, including their greatest prophet, Muhammad, not truly knowing if Allah will accept their good works as adequate. Their hearts know, although scared to challenge the faith of their family and friends, that what they believe does not bring the peace, or joy, or love that they yearn for.

Everyone desires oneness. With God and others.

20

Lordship and Humility

Humility often raises questions regarding parameters: "Am I supposed to become someone's doormat to just walk all over and let them get away with it?" Or, "How much of 'turning the other cheek' is too much? Seems like it encourages someone to become a bully." Finally, "Most people mistake humility for a weakness. Why not avoid the abuse by setting up some equitable boundaries?"

The preceding questions work on the misconception that humility is a character quality we implement when we deem it cost effective. As with all of Christ's character qualities, we don't pick and choose which to obey and when, we simply obey Him. Or, "Walking in the Spirit."

Living out Christ's humility, no different than all His nature, is directed by His Lordship. Let's take a deeper look at how looking to Jesus as Lord answers these questions (Luke 6:46-47).

Jesus didn't set His own reasonable parameters for humility; He obeyed His Father. "I only do and say what the Father tells me to do and say." Jesus went to the cross in obedience to His Father, not because mankind finally responded kindly to His message. Neither mankind's need nor mankind's response dictated how He loved or taught them, His Father did. Jesus kept the first commandment first. Reversing the two greatest commandments destroys both (Matthew 22:37-38; John 5:30).

Likewise, we make a love decision to submit to Christ's leading, not our own or others, or being needs-driven. What He wants us to give and to whom, we agree. How He wants us to serve and whom, we agree. We place ourselves under His authority for His purposes. "We live on Jesus' Island. To love Him, we put Him in charge of deciding how we love everyone and everything. We live holy as our love grows selfless."

Jesus may lead us to confront someone in authority as He turned the tables over in the temple, or serve someone grossly undeserving as He washed Judas' feet. We are not concerned with either the fear of confronting a person in authority or the embarrassment of serving a contemptible person because our focus remains on our obedience to Christ. We depend on Jesus in us, not us in us.

Nor does Jesus resist the person who just betrayed Him from kissing Him. As Jesus is, we grow to be, inexhaustible in humility. Only when we look to Him as Lord do we become Him, shedding all our natural limitations, and demanding our right to know.

....

This poses another question. If we become who Jesus is, then why do we see so many Christians and churches with different and sometimes opposing perspectives? One Christian acts extremely gracious while another speaks harshly to the same person and both remain certain they represent Christ. One pastor teaches grace when another speaks judgement out of the same Biblical text. Why the contradictions? Is Jesus schizophrenic?

The inconsistencies appear primarily because when we learn Who Jesus is, *we often fall in love with one or two qualities of His character, not His Lordship.*

Do we ask Christ, "How do You want me to respond in this person's life? Give them one more chance or lay down severe consequences?" Or, do we remain lord ourselves and pick and choose when and where to imitate our favorite qualities of Christ, not asking Him how He wants us to obey Him?

We all naturally favor certain aspects of Christ's life. Listed are a few:

Do you get excited when reading about how Jesus healed, raised the dead, and fed thousands of hungry folks, and want to do the same? Are you amazed at how Jesus flabbergasted the woman at the well by telling her of her five prior husbands? Good.

You may get excited about Jesus cleansing the temple and blasting the Pharisees for their sin. Perhaps you like how Jesus bluntly required the "rich young ruler" to sell his stuff because Jesus knew he loved his stuff more than Jesus. Good.

Or you may favor the Father's forgiveness in the prodigal son story and Jesus forgiving Mary Magdalene when the Pharisees wanted to stone her. Do you want to possess a heart of forgiveness like God's heart? Good.

Are Jesus' words, "Pick up your cross and follow Me," powerful to you? Does it amaze you how Jesus owned nothing and cared nothing of what others thought of Him? Does making personal sacrifices ring true to how you love God? Good.

How about Jesus never rubbing anyone's nose in their powerlessness, foolishness, or sin? He never gloated in His being the Creator of the Universe. Does that hidden and humble service resonate in your heart? Good.

It is easy to gravitate to one or two aspects of Christ's life while ignoring His lordship that incorporates all His attributes. Our lordship problem is betrayed when we focus on those areas that get us enthusiastic and neglect even learning those areas that sound less attractive to us. If we make Christ Lord, we recognize and guard our personal preferences. Then we will hear His voice directing us in every aspect of Who He is.

....

As stated, all these aspects of Christ's life accurately represent Him, but He did not pursue them specifically. Jesus willingly set aside His independent thinking and with a yielded heart Jesus followed His Father's lead in everything. Strictly speaking, Jesus didn't start with a mission to do miracles, judge, sacrifice, feed people, teach, and grieve for the lost. His mission was to obey His Father, Who directed Him when and where and for whom to do those things (Matthew 4:4).

Our stealthy pride reveals itself when we make self-directed sacrifices that expose our remaining in charge. Lucifer fell from heaven for wanting control, to be like the Most High. Large and in charge. His pride threw him out of heaven, no "nasty" evil. Averting God's Lordship constitutes the snare of Satan to Adam and Eve, "Don't you want to be as God?" (see Genesis 3:5; Isaiah 14:12-15).

Satan set up the same self-driven goodness entrapment for Jesus. After Jesus completed His wilderness fast, Satan tempted Him to take His eyes off His Father and to bring in His kingdom by feeding the hungry, doing miracles, and joining him to co-rule over mankind. Jesus didn't respond with, "Feeding people and doing miracles are evil." Or, "Who are you to offer Me a partnership?"

Nor did Satan tempt Jesus to do evil things such as lying, stealing, fornication or murder. Satan's temptation to Jesus was simply not to submit obeying His Father in His goodness. Christ's response always circled back to serving His Boss, not Himself or anyone else, "You shall worship the Lord your God, and Him only you shall serve" (Luke 4:8).

When not controlled by Christ's lordship, we will focus on a particular quality of Jesus and turn on our "Jesus show" where we become the star. True humility kicks out our independent spirit that once fell for Satan's temptations. *As humility made the difference in Christ's constant obedience to His Father, humility makes the difference for us to walk in oneness with Christ (Matthew 7:21-24).*

Back to the original concern, "When is it time to stop turning the other cheek? Humility must have limits."

When our hearts are sensitive to Christ's leading, we walk out what He has worked in and His infinite nature is never exhausted. Our focus is not on producing forgiveness, judging, making sacrifices, healing, wisdom, or even humbling ourselves. We don't favor and produce any one trait of Jesus; we simply favor serving Jesus.

....

All this leads to a telling lordship question. Is it possible for someone to truly live as one with Jesus, modeling all of Jesus' qualities while overlooking His humility?

Doing so remains impossible to conceive. Humility constitutes the essential state of heart that enables anyone to submit to Christ's Lordship over self-rule and provides the limitless power for each of His attributes to reach the anti-deserving.

When a self-driven churchgoer reads, "Give to those who steal from you" and "Bless those who curse you" and "Consider one another as more important than yourself" they know what Jesus said, but they don't believe He really means it literally for them. Their pride cannot obey those commands without feeling tortured. Their attempts to obey would drain their own shallow reservoir of love before breakfast. And Jesus cannot accept their independent attempts as true love for Him (First Corinthians 3:8-16).

Pride rationalizes that humility and the Sermon on the Mount remains Christ's "idealistic" or "poetic" teachings. Or maybe those teachings are just for super-saints in special situations. "Life can't be continuously lived under those principles. Forgive seventy times seven? That's only going to make life hell for everyone. Jesus must mean forgive some people more than you want to."

Our self-governing directs us to use filters and defaults to what goodness our pride agrees to. "Jesus loves everyone. I am going to volunteer to feed the homeless. But I won't work alongside brother George because he offended me last month. And, I am not going to feed anyone that I know is a sex offender. Two hours of my precious time will more than suffice. I can do this if I focus on the job, not the smelly people with bad oral hygiene."

We become our own "trophy" when our self-ruled service takes our eyes off Christ's humility and focuses on performing one aspect of His goodness. When a self-ruled person reads about Jesus' signs and wonders, they will naturally think of themselves making a big splash "for God." Their eyes come off the Miracle Worker and onto the miracle, and what they will do to impress God and others.

When a proud person reads of Jesus' strong judgements, they get on their high horse and look down their noses at those less righteous than themselves. When an independent person reads of His sacrifice, they think of how to make the most impressive sacrifice to prove their devotion to God, when in fact they are looking for applause from others. Everything Godly turns godless with pride. Selfless love turns selfish. "Look at how charitable I am to these very undeserving folks!" (see First Corinthians 13:1-3).

"But when you do a charitable deed, do not let your left hand know what your right hand is doing." Matthew 6:3

Only humbling down enables someone to willingly shift their lordship from themselves to Christ. Then He loves, heals, gives, and judges through us, and we look to His lead in knowing what's next. *Pride, in order to stay in control, rushes past listening to Jesus and chases loving, healing, giving, and judging themselves.*

If we pursue the goodness of God without first submitting to His leading, our natural thinking will take over and we will necessarily mishandle His goodness for our benefit, insisting on certain results. We start thinking we can use His goodness like a fix-all tool. We diagnose the problem ourselves and then choose the right tool to fix it.

For example, let's say someone comes to you with financial problems. Your natural diagnosis is, "They need to increase their income." Your self-driven kindness states, "More schooling will land them a better paying job. I will even help with the costs."

But first asking Christ what He sees as the problem, He answers, "They need more self-control in their spending."

Or, "They self-sabotage their lives to avoid responsibility." Then you ask, "What is Your solution?" He answers, "I want you to disciple them." His answer requires humbly loving them and maturity in your own life.

Nothing opens one's spiritual ears to hear God's voice like humility. Ask Christ, "Who am I trusting? Who initiates my goodness? Whose praise am I seeking? Who is beneath me? Who receives the credit? Who does the outcome matter to? Why do I stress?" Ask God to reveal your heart to yourself so you can pray with no heart of your own in the matter. If we possess anxiety, frustration, concern for others' approval, etc., when serving God, it begs the question if our pride has something to do with it.

Probably the most obvious red flag that a Christian remains self-driven in their favorite qualities of Jesus is their resistance to submit to those in authority. Not having been "Jesus humbled" time and time again through the process of getting their attitudes corrected in prayer by Jesus, they still hold a high opinion of their own opinion. Not having listened and then obeyed Jesus' leading over their own, they don't possess the secondary "skill" to yield to authority. *If the devil can't get you to stop your goodness, he will tempt you to go it alone (Romans 12:3).*

....

Once again, we feel overwhelmed, *"But I thought the nature of Christ flowed out of us naturally. This sounds more like drudgery, trying to figure out the difference between my heart and His heart on every little detail in life."*

Christ flows out of us when we walk in spiritual oneness with Him. Sadly, our pride and the world snuck many ungodly patterns of thinking into our minds that we remain oblivious to. These hidden, but ungodly thoughts, must be exposed by the Holy Spirit to know they exist and to replace them with Christ's thoughts.

A humble person willfully accepts the challenge of the Holy Spirit weeding out prideful thinking. They want oneness at any cost. Only pride puts the "drudgery" in "search my heart oh God." Pride makes the "narrow road" narrow and difficult. If we lost our pride and walked in Christ's humility, today's church would experience the same oneness as the church after Pentecost (Matthew 7:14; Acts 2:46-47).

In a nutshell, how do we become Jesus with "skin on?" We must make the humble decision to keep our hearts "walking on its knees" before Jesus. We enjoy "come to Jesus" picnics instead of religiously following "black ink on white paper," or our own hearts. Then we will love our lives as He leads and flows through us. If we take our eyes off Jesus and put them on our favorite qualities of His, we will lose His joy as we try to control and insist on certain outcomes.

....

Imagine the struggle Jesus would have faced had He taken His eyes off pleasing His Father and put them on those He served? He would have been incredibly disheartened by their moments of foolishness and sin. If we experience crippling discouragement in loving others, who are we serving (Matthew 20:23; John 14:9)?

When our eyes are focused on Christ, what others do or say can't sidetrack us from pleasing Him. What matters to us is what Jesus gives to us. His worthiness. His praise. His purposes. Looking around us will stir up storms in our souls and derail us. Looking to Jesus we enjoy peace and living one with Him. *Agape love is never wasted.* "Do all in the name of the Lord" (Colossians 3:17).

Practically speaking, to get "Jesus humble" we ask, "Jesus, how are You best served in this person's life?" Then wait for what He impresses on our hearts. Turn the other cheek or admonish? Let the money go or pursue payment? Whatever Jesus directs, "give them your coat also" or "time to throw over a table," He gives us His love and power to obey. "My sheep hear My voice, and I know them, and they follow Me" (John 10:27).

Acknowledgments

As a doctor learns medicine by practicing on sick people, I learned the Biblical principles presented in this book by counseling thousands of broken people over a twenty-five-year span. I am grateful to them for their patience with me as God sharpened my understanding of His truths.

Unquestionably, my wife, Cindy, receives the "most patient" award. She gently counseled me all along the way, often on our long evening walks. Thank you, Cynthia, for forty-one beautiful years of marriage and for your words of wisdom on so many issues that confronted me throughout our marriage and ministry.

About the Author

After graduating from business college and seminary, Bjorn, and his wife, Cindy, opened and operated a successful restaurant for ten years, located in Southern California.

When hearing God say, "Time to quit feeding people's stomachs and start feeding their souls," they sold the restaurant in 1996 and shortly after opened a large long-term shelter that houses people who are going through a devastating crisis and want to turn their lives over to God.

This book represents twenty-five years of hard-fought wisdom, often received through listening prayer, and heavily influenced by Bjorn's favorite authors, Oswald Chambers and C. S. Lewis.

Practically speaking, Bjorn has lived with and counseled thousands of people who have wrestled with physical and sexual abuse, addictions, anger, suicide, demonic oppression, anxiety, etc. His writings seek out the heart of God to tackle spiritual issues while illustrating Biblical truths using everyday illustrations

www.ingramcontent.com/pod-product-compliance
Lightning Source LLC
LaVergne TN
LVHW041541070426
835507LV00011B/863